Rationale Divinorum Officiorum
by Guillaume Durandus

Volume One
A modern translation of
Author's Preface and Book One

Translated by

Janet Gentles

Paschal Light

Copyright © 2019 Janet Gentles

All rights reserved.

ISBN: 978-1-913017-01-9

Contents

PREFACE TO VOLUME ONE	i
TRANSLATOR'S INTRODUCTION TO VOLUME ONE	iii
GUILLAUME DURANDUS'S PREFACE	1
BOOK ONE	1
1 THE CHURCH AND ITS PARTS	13
2 THE ALTAR	33
3 PICTURES, CURTAINS AND CHURCH ORNAMENTS	42
4 THE BELLS	66
5 CEMETERIES AND OTHER SACRED AND RELIGIOUS PLACES	73
6 THE DEDICATION OF THE CHURCH	80
7 THE DEDICATION OF THE ALTAR	101
8 CONSECRATIONS AND UNCTIONS	117
9 THE SACRAMENTS OF THE CHURCH	132
SCRIPTURE INDEX	139
SUBJECT INDEX	147

PREFACE TO VOLUME ONE

Janet Gentles has been known to me for many years as a woman with wide-ranging and deep spiritual interests. Her passion for spiritual insight has taken her, not into realms of imaginative speculations or trendy practices, but into an examination of the spiritual depths of the Church's historic liturgy and the ancient traditions of the Jewish and Christian faiths.

When she became aware of the work of Guillaume Durandus, *Rationale Divinorum Officiorum*, she felt that here was a project that needed to be done—translating and publishing this entire work in an accessible format in English. She has translated and edited the entire eight books, organized into six volumes with a further volume of indices, providing such helps for the reader as biblical references, historical notes, and sometimes preliminary comments on her own understanding of what Durandus is saying. This is not intended to be a work of historical scholarship, although I suspect that many scholars of liturgy and medieval history will find it useful. Rather, Gentles has produced an accurate and user-friendly English version that serves to introduce this work of Durandus to a wider audience. She believes that it will appeal to anyone who is interested in probing more deeply into the spiritual wisdom and practice of the high medieval flowering of spirituality in Western Christianity. I believe that she has indeed produced an accurate rendering that will introduce Durandus's work to many who are on a spiritual journey and seek symbolic meaning in the church and liturgy that can escape the notice of casual worshippers.

Durandus directed his work especially to priests who, in his opinion, were not aware of the spiritual significance of the buildings, furnishings, liturgy, and other practices that they were in charge of tending and performing. In some ways, he produced an encyclopaedic compendium of the traditions of the church pertaining to these matters, with copious quotations from ecclesial writers, especially St Augustine, and various Popes and Church Councils. But this is also a work in which Durandus applied his spiritual insights to all these matters, with rich biblical references and attention not only to the historical meaning but also to figurative meaning.

I commend this translation for its accuracy, for its appreciation for the (often rather esoteric) assertion of symbolic meanings, and above all for the footnotes that list the biblical references and contain historical information about Popes and Councils and theologians. She is also willing to point out places where Durandus is apparently mistaken in such things as etymologies of words, since his knowledge of Greek and Eastern Church traditions was limited.

In this first volume, containing Book One of the *Rationale*, Durandus first explains his purposes and procedures, then discusses the church building, its furnishings, and the ceremonies that relate to these things. I hope that the hard work of Janet Gentles in producing this translation will be rewarded by the appreciation of those who read it.

Rev. Dr. David Kuck
Lecturer in New Testament
United Theological College of the West Indies
Kingston, Jamaica

TRANSLATOR'S INTRODUCTION TO VOLUME ONE

Towards the end of the thirteenth century Guillaume Durandus (or William Durand), Bishop of Mende, compiled the eight books which constitute his *Rationale Divinorum Officiorum* or 'Rationale of the Divine Offices', a work which has remained highly esteemed since that time. His aim in preparing this work was to instruct both the clergy and the faithful. Books One and Three were (rather poorly) translated into English in the latter part of the nineteen century and it is indeed unfortunate that the entire work has been unavailable to English readers until current times.

The Life of Guillaume Durandus

Durandus was born in or around 1230 in Beziers, southern France, into a prominent family which provided him with an excellent education. This instruction would have included a considerable emphasis on both canon and civil law as there was a popular emphasis on these subjects at that time. By the age of twenty-four he was a canon regular of the cathedral of Maguelone and a cleric of the church of Narbonne. A year later he was in Paris where he attended lessons at the university for a short period before moving to Italy to further his studies in law. This led to his achieving the rank of Doctor of Canon Law and he gained such a reputation for knowledge and talent that he was given the responsibilities of teaching the law at Bologna and then at Modena.

In 1265, when he was thirty-four years of age, and still growing in reputation, he was called by Pope Clement IV to the functions of apostolic chaplain and auditor general of the sacred palace. It was at that same time he was provided with two honorary canonicals, one in the Cathedral of Beauvais, the other in that of Narbonne.

During this period our author was compiling his principle work, the *Speculum Judiciale*, a general explanation of civil, criminal and canonical procedure, which was published in 1271.

After the death of Pope Clement IV and the election of his successor, Pope Gregory X, Durandus was attached to the pontifical court, and attended the Second Council of Lyons. Being reputed for his work on law, he was among the prelates who drew up the constitutions resulting from this assembly. He refers to this event particularly in Book Four of the *Rationale*.

The following years saw Durandus embroiled in the political struggles. These include the defence of papal territories, not only by the use of diplomacy but also of arms. That such an outstanding cleric should be connected with warfare may seem surprising but, as Durandus himself wrote, 'A cleric may be in charge of the conduct of a just war, not to command directly men of blood, but to respond to the soldiers, provide the money, hold the treaties, make sentences, dispose all things, as we ourselves have done in the war which the Church of Rome has supported in Romagna against cities in revolt.'

The *Rationale Divinorum Officiorum*, was published in 1284 and he was elected Bishop of Mende in 1286 but remained in Italy until 1291.

Durandus, who had been called to Rome in the interests of the Church, died in that city on the 1st of November, 1296. His funeral rites and entombment were in the Dominican church of the Minerva, in Rome.

Spirituality of the Rationale

It should not be supposed that the extensive contents of the eight books which comprise the *Rationale* are entirely the work of one man. Rather it brings together in summary the greater part of what had been learned and understood, with mind and heart, by the Fathers, Doctors, and scholars who had written about the liturgy from the beginning of Christianity. Durandus presents and comments on these elucidations with as much clarity as depth, demonstrating a great knowledge, style, and logic. So much so that the *Rationale Divinorum Officiorum* has been called the '13th Century Liturgical Encyclopaedia.' Yet spiritual truths are immutable. The way that they are represented may vary slightly with changing times and in various cultures but the spiritual principles the outer form refers to does not, or should not, change. The result is that this work could well still be called a 'Liturgical Encyclopaedia' today as there is comparatively little in it which should be confined to the pages of history.

When engaging with the *Rationale* it is beneficial to bear several things in mind. The first is that Christianity is unquestionably concerned with the path of spiritual growth or development. It is a journey which leads into an ever closer encounter with God through Christ. The second is that while there are many books on spiritual theology these almost invariable look at the individual experience of development rather than how the Offices of the Church nurture this development. The *Rationale* is arguably the most comprehensive book of this nature.

The third point is that it adopts the perspective, perhaps too little appreciated today, that spiritual development can be seen not only as vertical path of ascent but also linearly as a progression through time. St Augustine explains this in his *Enchiridion*:

> *When, sunk in the darkest depths of ignorance, man lives according to the flesh undisturbed by any struggle of reason or conscience, this is his first state. Afterwards, when through the law he has come the knowledge of sin, and the Spirit of God has not yet interposed His aid, man, striving to live according to the law, is thwarted in his efforts and falls into conscious sin, and so, being overcome of sin, becomes its slave.*[1] *Thus the effect produced by the knowledge of the commandment is this, that sin works in man all manner of lustfulness, and he is involved in the additional guilt of wilful transgression, and that is fulfilled which is written: 'the law entered, that the offence might abound'.*[2] *This is man's second state. But if God has regard to him, and inspires him*

---

[1] See 2 Peter 2:19
[2] Romans 5:20

with faith in God's help, and the Spirit of God begins to work in him, then the mightier power of love strives against the power of the flesh. However although there is still in the man's own nature a power that fights against him (for his disease is not completely cured), yet he lives the life of the just by faith, and lives in righteousness so far as he does not yield to evil lust, but conquers it by the love of holiness. This is the third state of a man of good hope; and he who by steadfast piety advances in this course, shall attain at last to peace, that peace which, after this life is over, shall be perfected in the repose of the spirit, and finally in the resurrection of the body. Of these four different stages the first is before the law, the second is under the law, the third is under grace, and the fourth is in full and perfect peace. Thus, too, has the history of God's people been ordered according to His pleasure…For the church existed at first before the law; then under the law, which was given by Moses; then under grace, which was first made manifest in the coming of the Mediator.

The fourth point is one should not easily dismiss things which appear either trite or obscure. With regards to things which may appear trite, an example can be found in Book One where Durandus sees the cock on the pinnacle of the church as representing the crowing of the preacher. This makes far more sense when we consider his likely source, namely, *The Book of Pastoral Rule*, of Gregory the Great:

> *But the preacher should know how to avoid drawing the mind of his hearer beyond its strength, lest, so to speak, the string of the soul, when stretched more than it can bear, should be broken. For all deep things should be covered up before a multitude of hearers, and scarcely opened to a few. For hence the Truth in person says, 'Who then is that faithful and wise steward, whom his lord shall make ruler over his household, to give them their portion of meat in due season?*[3] *Now by a measure of wheat is expressed a portion of the Word, lest, when anything is given to a narrow heart beyond its capacity, it be spilt. Hence Paul says, 'And I, brethren, could not speak unto you as unto spiritual, but as unto carnal, even as unto babes in Christ. I have fed you with milk, and not with meat: for hitherto ye were not able to*

---

[3] Luke 12:42

> *bear it, neither yet now are ye able.*[4] *Hence Moses, when he comes on from the sanctuary of God, veils his shining face before the people; because in truth He does not show to the multitudes the secrets of inmost brightness.*[5]
>
> *But the cock is inclined to utter loud chants in the deeper hours of the night; but, when the time of morning is already at hand, he frames small and slender tones. Because, in fact, he who preaches correctly cries aloud plainly to hearts that are still in the dark, and shows them nothing of hidden mysteries, that they may then hear the more subtle teachings concerning heavenly things, when they draw nigh to the light of truth.*

With regards to things that are obscure, one should not dismiss things which appear to be incomprehensible or for which only a partial explanation is provided. Many Church Fathers refer to this. Here is what Origen says to Gregory:[6]

> *While you attend to this divine reading seek properly and with unwavering faith in God the hidden sense which is present in most passages of the divine Scriptures. And do not be content with knocking and seeking, for what is most necessary for understanding divine things is prayer, and in urging us to this the Saviour says not only, 'Knock, and it shall be opened to you,' and 'Seek, and ye shall find,' but also 'Ask, and it shall be given you.'*[7]

While one can comfortably read each book of the Rationale from cover to cover at the end of each there will undoubtedly remain the awareness that a great deal has been missed. There are countless topics to consider and insights to be gained in this incredible work which can not only serve to enhance liturgical worship but also one's spiritual understanding and personal development.

---

[4] 1 Corinthians 3:1-2
[5] See Exodus 34:33, 35
[6] Origen was writing to the young Gregory, Thaumaturgus who was later to become bishop of Caesarea
[7] See Matthew 5:7-8, Luke 11:9-10

VOLUME ONE

This Translation

In this translation, which is intended to be used more for its spiritual content rather than a resource for detailed historical study, specific references to the numerous sources the author drew from have been omitted. He sometimes paraphrases biblical quotations and here either a reference to the relevant text is given or a direct quotation from the King James Version (KJV) is incorporated. In instances where the book referred to is not found in the KJV the quotation is from the Vulgate. In cases where the Vulgate translation (which Durandus would have used) is more explanatory, the KJV wording is given in the text and the Vulgate provided in the relevant footnote. These multitudinal quotations add yet another element to this multidimensional work, for the explanation that Durandus provides can offer further insight into biblical text the quotation is taken from.

The *Divine Rationale Divinorum Officiorum* consists of eight books. In this translation these have been presented in six volumes with a seventh volume of indices. The following list will be found at the end of each volume for easy reference.

Volume 1
Author's Preface
Book 1 - The Church and its Parts

Volume 2
Book 2 - Ministers, ecclesiastical dignities and their duties
Book 3 - The Sacred Vestments

Volume 3
Book 4 - The Mass and its Mysteries

Volume 4
Book 5 - The Divine Offices

Volume 5
Book 6 - The Liturgical Year

TRANSLATOR'S INTRODUCTION TO VOLUME ONE

Volume 6
Book 7 - The Festivals of Saints Book
8 - Computation and the Calendar

Volume 7 – Indices

Finally I would like to thank Rev. Dr. David Kuck for his encouragement and advice from the beginning of this project, for writing the prefaces of each volume and for his assistance with the ancient Greek. My thanks also to Mary Kuck for her many hours of skilful proofreading.

GUILLAUME DURANDUS'S PREFACE

1. All things belonging to the Offices, customs, or ornaments of the Church are full of divine figures and mysteries. Each of these, in particular, is overflowing with a celestial sweetness; when they encounter a man who examines them with attention and love, and who knows how 'to suck honey out of the rock, and oil out of the flinty rock.'[8] However, 'Knowest thou the ordinances of heaven? canst thou set the dominion thereof in the earth?'[9] Certainly, whoever wishes to scrutinize His majesty would be crushed by His glory; for it is a deep well. I have nothing with which to draw from it,[10] unless He who gives to all abundantly, and without admonishing them,[11] presents me with the necessary vessel. Then I may drink with joy, from the fountains of the Saviour, the water which flows from the midst of the mountains[12] But, we cannot give the reason for all that has been transmitted to us by our ancestors, since it is necessary to remove what has no foundation. That is why I, Guillaume Durandus, appointed bishop of the holy Church of Mende, by the sole permission of God, will knock and I will not cease from knocking at the door. Perhaps 'the key of David'[13] will consent to open it to me, so that the king may introduce me into the cellar where He keeps His wine.[14] There also the divine model which was shown to Moses

---

[8] Deuteronomy 32:13
[9] Job 38:33
[10] See John 4:11
[11] See James 1:5
[12] See Psalm 104:10 and Isaiah 12:3
[13] Revelation 3:7
[14] See Song of Songs 2:4

on the mountain[15] will be revealed to me, until I can explain in clear and precise terms what is signified, and what is contained in all things which relate to the Offices, usages, or ornaments of the Church. Then I may fix their rules; after it has been revealed to me by Him who makes the children's tongues speak,[16] and whose spirit 'bloweth where it listeth',[17] 'dividing to every man severally as he will,'[18] for the praise and glory of the Trinity.

2. Here we take the sacraments as signs or figures, but these figures are not the virtues, but the signs of the virtues, and are used as a written word to teach them. As for these signs, some are simple, others practical. This matter will be discussed further in Book Four of this work, under the chapter *The Seventh Part of the Canon*, where the mystery of faith is considered.

3. Now the priests and prelates of the Church,[19] to whom 'it is given to know the mysteries of the kingdom of God,'[20] and who are the distributors and dispensers of the sacraments, must have the integrity of the sacraments and shine with the virtues they represent, so that by their brilliance others may be enlightened and illuminated. Without this they are 'blind leaders of the blind,'[21] and, according to the words of the prophet, 'their eyes be darkened, that they see not.'[22] Nonetheless, sadly, there are many today who have little understanding of things of daily use which relate to the practices of the Church and serve in the Offices, yet do not know what they mean, or why they were instituted. Here the word of the prophet appears to be literally fulfilled, 'as with the people, so with the priest.'[23] They bear the loaves of the offering and celebrate the mysteries at the table of the Lord without understanding or looking at them; so that, without doubt, they will be regarded by the righteous judgement

---

[15] See Deuteronomy 5:4
[16] See Wisdom 10:21
[17] John 3:8
[18] 1 Corinthians 12:11
[19] Spiritually this means those who have made considerable progress on the spiritual journey
[20] Luke 8:1
[21] Matthew 15:14
[22] Psalm 69:23
[23] Isaiah 24:2

of God as beasts of burden carrying food that others are meant to eat. They will have to account for this ignorance on the day of vengeance and anger; and as the cedars of paradise tremble, what shall the reed of the wilderness do? For they were told by the prophet, 'they have not known my ways: Unto whom I sware in my wrath that they should not enter into my rest.'[24]

4. Now the professors of the liberal arts, whoever they may be, make every effort to put the things contained in these arts in a naked and perhaps colourless manner and try to colour them, to embellish them. Painters, too, and all men, artisans or workmen, apply themselves to details of every kind, to give of their profession or of their plausible reasons and causes, and to have these on the spot. Also, according to the laws of the world, it is shameful for a patrician and an advocate to ignore the law, in which he ought to have a great deal of knowledge of since he wishes to make this the occupation of his whole life.

5. At the same time, although spiritual knowledge is very necessary for the priests since they are destined to teach others, ignorant priests should not be considered less than teachers of schoolroom knowledge, according to this from Exodus, 'Thou shalt not revile the gods, nor curse the ruler of thy people.'[25] Therefore, according to St Augustine, we should not laugh if we happen to hear some bishops and ministers of the Church invoke God in barbaric or distorted terms, or if it is perceived that they do not even understand the words they pronounce and that they only murmur them confusedly. Those who observe this must not blame those people, but they must tolerate them with charity and goodness. As to what the priests ought to know, we shall explain in Book Two of this work, in the chapter *The Priest*.

6. Many do not see that what takes place in the customs and Offices of the Church is done in a figurative sense, because the meaning of the symbols has been forgotten, and it is now the time of truth, and because we ought not to be like the Jews. Now although some of the symbolic meaning by which truth has been revealed has been lost today, still many truths which we do not perceive nevertheless remain hidden in the shadow, and that is

---

[24] Psalm 95:10-11
[25] Exodus 22:28

why the Church still uses figures. Thus, by the white vestments, we understand in some way the beauty of our souls, that is to say, the glory of our immortality, which we cannot see clearly. In the Mass, and before the Preface, we represent the preliminaries of the Passion of Christ, so that the circumstances of this fact may be imprinted more firmly and faithfully in the memory.

7. It is to be observed that of the things which are contained in the law, some are moral, others mystical. The moral are those which form morals, and they are to be understood as the words themselves express them, as for example, 'Thou shalt not take the name of the Lord thy God in vain…Honour thy father and thy mother…Thou shalt not kill, etc.'[26] Mystical things are figurative things which signify something other than what the letter of the word says. Of these mystical things, some are sacramental, others ceremonial. The sacramentals are those for which a reason can be given; that is why they must be observed to the letter, such as circumcision, the observance of the Sabbath, and other things of this kind. On the other hand, ceremonials are those which we cannot account for, because they are according to precept, as by for example, 'Thou shalt not sow thy vineyard with divers seeds…Thou shalt not plow with an ox and an ass together. Thou shalt not wear a garment of divers sorts, as of woollen and linen together.'[27] and such things.

8. Also, with regard in moral things, the law does not undergo any change; but, with regard to sacramental and ceremonial things, there has only been a slight change in inconsequential ways; but yet their mystical sense has not changed. Therefore it is not said that the law is changed, although it has been transplanted into us by the priesthood.[28]

9. We must also know that in the divine scriptures there are the historical, allegorical, tropological and anagogical senses. Therefore, according to Boethius, all divine authority is placed; either in the historical, in the allegorical, or in both senses. Also, according to St Jerome, we must examine the divine scripture in three ways: firstly according to the letter; secondly, according to

---

[26] Exodus 20:7-17
[27] Deuteronomy 22:11
[28] See Hebrews 7:12

allegory, that is, the spiritual sense; third, according to the felicity of the eternal life. History is the meaning of speech attached to things; for instance, whenever a fact is reported wholly as it happened in the letter, for example, how the Israelite people, saved from Egypt, made and erected a temple to the Lord.[29] The word 'history' comes from a Greek word *historía* which means to express a thing by gestures, and that is why historians are called *histriones*, gesticulators, like the *histrions*, 'actors'.[30]

10. Allegory exists when a word produces a sound whose meaning is different in the mind, as when by one fact one has the understanding of another. If the object designated by the word is visible, it is simply an allegory; if it is invisible and celestial, then it is called anagogy. It is also an allegory when, by a foreign phrase, a foreign state is expressed, as when the presence of Christ or the sacraments of the Church are designated by words or mystical things; for example, as in this place, 'there shall come forth a rod out of the stem of Jesse, and a Branch shall grow out of his roots.'[31] This is understood to mean that the Virgin Mary will be born of the race of David, who was the son of Jesse. As for the mystical things, for example, the people delivered from Egyptian slavery by the blood of the Lamb. This means that the Church was torn from the slavery of the devil by the Passion of Christ. Now the word 'allegory' comes from a Greek word *alios* which means 'other', and *goro*[32] which means 'senses', as if to say 'a foreign meaning' or 'a different sense.'

---

[29] See Exodus 36

[30] Here Durandus conveys the idea of a story-teller rather than a historian.. The Greek *historia* means 'learning through research] or 'narration of what is learned'. In his day the Greek language was then almost unknown in the schools of the west, and Durandus was not more ignorant in this than many others; so he cannot be blamed for speaking of what he did not know. He makes several errors in both the Latin and Greek etymologies he gives. There was also the tendency with Durandus, like his predecessors and the authors who followed him in the fourteenth century, that when he found difficulty in finding the true origin of a word he put the quest aside to find those features of light which would dazzle the reader; like the spark that springs from the pebble

[31] Isaiah 11:1

[32] It seems *agoreuo* is intended

11. The Greek word *tropologia*, tropology is the conversion of discourse to morals, or a way of moral speech to correct and to form manners; and it can be considered in two ways, mystical or clear. In a mystical way, as in this text, 'Let thy garments be always white; and let thy head lack no ointment.'[33] that is to say, 'May your works be pure, and let charity never come out of your soul.' Also, 'David must kill Goliath for us,'[34] that is, 'Let humility kill pride.' In a clear way, as here, 'If thine enemy be hungry, give him bread to eat,'[35] and in this other place, 'let us not love in word, neither in tongue; but in deed and in truth.'[36] The word 'tropology'[37] comes from the Greek *tropos* which means 'conversion' or 'change,' and from *logos* which means 'word,' as if one were saying 'a word changed.'

12. 'Anagogy'[38] (or *anagoge*) comes from the Greek words *ana* which is 'upwards' and *goge*, 'a leading,' as if to say 'direction upwards.' It is called this because the anagogical sense leads from things that are visible to things which are invisible. Thus, for instance, light made on the first day means the invisible thing, that is, the angelic nature created in the beginning. Anagogy is therefore the expression of a sense that leads to heavenly things, or to the Church which is above, namely to the Trinity and the orders of angels, and speaks, through clear or mystical discourses, of the future reward and the life to come which is in heaven. A clear example is 'Blessed are the pure in heart: for they shall see God.'[39] A mystical example is, blessed are those who, 'have washed their robes, and made them white in the blood of the Lamb,'[40] 'that they may have right to the tree of life, and may enter in through the gates into the city.'[41] This means clearly: blessed are those who purify their thoughts, because they will have the

---

[33] Ecclesiastes 9:8
[34] See 1 Samuel 17:48-50
[35] Proverbs 25:21
[36] 1 John 3:18
[37] The figurative interpretation of the scriptures as a source of moral guidance
[38] A method of mystical or spiritual interpretation of scripture
[39] Matthew 5:8
[40] Revelation 7:14
[41] Revelation 22:14

power to see God, who is the way, the truth and the life,[42] and that, by doctrine, that is to say by the example of the Fathers, they will enter the kingdom of heaven. In the same way, Jerusalem signifies historically the terrestrial city of this name, where pilgrims go, and allegorically it is the militant Church, and tropologically any faithful soul; finally, anagogically, Jerusalem or the heavenly homeland. We can see other examples regarding these things in the lessons we read on Holy Saturday, as we will read in Book Six. Now, in this work, most of the time the same various meanings are used, and one passes alternately from one to the other, as the diligent reader can see clearly.

13. For just as no one is prohibited from using views of exceptions or types of defences, so he is not forbidden to explain, in praise of God, the ceremonies of the Church in different ways, provided, however, that the faith remains unaffected.

14. It must be considered, in fact, that a large number of different usages are found in the celebration of divine worship. In fact, almost every church has its own and proper observances. Nor is it reprehensible or absurd to venerate God and His saints by various concerts or modulations and by different observances. This is so because the Church Triumphant herself, according to the prophet, is adorned with garments of various colours, and that, in the very administration of the sacraments of the Church, the variety of ceremonies is tolerated by the law of custom.

15. This led St Augustine to say that of the teachings of the Church on the Divine Office we have received some from scripture, others from the Apostolic Tradition, which are outside the scriptures and which have been confirmed by the successors of the Apostles. Others, also have been fortified by custom; and in these, however, the institution has been ignored, but they have been approved by custom, and so obedience or observance is due to them.

16. Therefore the reader will not be astonished if he happens to read in this guide something he does not know to be observed in his Church, or if he does not find what is observed there. In fact, we do not deal here with special things in every place, but the common and most used rites; for we have resolved to expound

---

[42] See John 14:6

on the common doctrine and not the particular, and it is not possible for us to seek out and examine the special things of any particular country. That is why we have decided, for the sake of our souls and for the usefulness of the readers, to reveal and explain here, as far as we will be able, and in a clear style, the hidden mysteries of the Divine Offices, also to clarify what seemed to us necessary to be understood by ecclesiastics for their daily use, and to explain it intimately, by penetrating to the marrow of the subject. This, as we know, I formerly did in the *Speculum Judiciale*, for the use of those who judge the affairs of this world, men placed in a state which is quite different from the first.
17. Nevertheless, one must be careful that, as far as even the Divine Offices are concerned, there are several ceremonies of observance which, by their origin, do not relate to either the moral sense or the mystical sense.[43] Some of these are because of necessity, some for reasons of convenience, others because of the difference between the old and the new law, some for their expediency; others, finally, to give more honour and reverence to the celebration of the Divine Offices, which are known to have passed into the state of custom. It is for this reason, as Blessed Augustine says, that the ceremonies of different countries vary infinitely, according to the diversity of traditions and usages; so that it is scarcely, or never entirely, that we can find the causes that determined men to establish and observe them.
18. Now, this book is called *Rationale*; for, just as in the rational of judgment which the High Priest of the law bore upon his breast,[44] it was written, 'Manifestation and truth.'[45] Thus in this work the reasons for the various ceremonies in the Divine Offices, and their varieties, are clearly described and revealed, and the prelates and priests of the churches are to keep them faithfully in the box

---

[43] This passage is worth noting, as showing that our Author does not proceed with the determination of making a meaning where he could not find one but that he is willing to leave much, explained only in the principles of necessity, or convenience, or reverence

[44] See Exodus 28:4

[45] Exodus 28:30 *Urim* means 'lights' and metaphorically 'revelation' or 'revelations.' *Thummim* means 'perfection' or 'complete Truth.' So these stones on the breastplate represent the spiritual light of the most profound revelations which a priest should carry in his heart

of their hearts. Now on that rationale[46] there was a stone by the brightness of which the sons of Israel knew when God would be propitious to them. In the same way, the devout reader, being instructed by the splendour of this reading in the mysteries of the Divine Offices, will recognize that God will be propitious to us. Providing however, that we do not incur His indignation by the unforeseen injury of a sin. This rationale was also a cloth made of four colours and with gold threads and so is the structure of this book. For in it (as has been said above), are the reasons for the variety in the usages of the Church and in the Offices and why they are adorned with different colours. For the four senses can be found there, namely, the historical, the allegorical, the tropological and the anagogical, and finally by the faith which is in the middle of these four kinds of colours.

19. Finally, this work is divided into eight distinct parts, which we will follow, in their order, with the help of the Lord. Of which, the first will deal with the Church and the places which depend on it, her ornaments, her consecration and the sacraments. The second, ministers of the Church and their offices. The third, the sacerdotal and other vestments. The fourth, on the Mass and all the ceremonies of the Mass. The fifth of the other Divine Offices, in general. The sixth will deal with all Sundays, holidays and festivities dedicated to the Lord. The seventh, with the festivities of the saints, and the festival and the Offices of the Dedication of the Church and the Dead. The eighth, with the method of computing time and the calendar

END OF AUTHOR'S PREFACE

---

[46] Or Breastplate

BOOK ONE

1 THE CHURCH AND ITS PARTS

1. The first thing we need to look at is what concerns the Church and its parts. We must, therefore, observe, concerning churches, that one is the material building, namely, that in which the Divine Offices are celebrated; the other is spiritual. The spiritual church is the congregation of the faithful or the people summoned by the ministers of Christ and gathered together in one place by the one who causes all those who profess the same worship and the same sentiments to live in His house.[47] Now just as the corporeal or material church is built of stones joined together; so, the spiritual church forms a whole composed of a large number of men of different ages and ranks.

2. The Greek word *ekklesia* is in Latin *ecclesia* and means 'convocation, or 'assembly,' because the Church calls all everyone to her. This name is more appropriately suited to the spiritual Church than to the material church; because people are assembled and convoked (called together), and not stones. However, it often happens that the name of the thing represented is attributed to its representation, and the material church represents the spiritual church, as will be said when we treat of its consecration. The word *ecclesia*, also signifies that the Church is Catholic, that is, universal. This is because it is established or spread by the whole world, and because all who believe in God must meet in the same assembly, or because the Catholic Church has in it a universal doctrine for the instruction of all the faithful.

3. Again, synagogue, comes from the Greek word *sunagoge* which means assembly, and this name was peculiar to the Jewish people. Their place of worship is usually called a synagogue, although this name has sometimes been applied to a church. Yet the Apostles

---

[47] See Psalm 68:6

never called the meeting place of the faithful by the name of synagogue, but always the church, and this was perhaps to distinguish them from each other.

4. The Church Militant[48] is called 'Zion,' because, on account of the pilgrimage of this life, placed far from the promise of heavenly joys, people await it and contemplate it, and this is why it has received the name of Zion, that is, 'waiting.' Then, because of the country and the peace to come to which the Church tends (*i.e.* the Church Triumphant), it is called 'Jerusalem;' because Jerusalem is interpreted 'vision of peace.' The church is also called the House of God, *Domus Dei*, and this name comes from the Greek word *diogmate*,[49] which means 'right,' as if it were meant to express that God grants to mankind the grace of remain united by the same feelings within it. It is also sometimes called *kuria*, that is to say, belonging to the Lord. At times the Latin word 'basilica' is used, (*basilike* in Greek), which means 'the palace of the king,' that is to say, the royal dwelling; and the palaces of the kings of the earth are called this. However, our house, which is a house of prayer, is called a royal dwelling, because in its enclosure one comes to pay his court to the King of Kings. Sometimes the church is called the temple, *templum*, as if it were called a broad and extended roof, *tectum amplum*, from which we offer sacrifices to God our King, or it may be referred to as a tabernacle or tent of God, *Dei tabernaculum*. This is because on this earth our present life is a pilgrimage and that it is marching towards the lasting country, as will soon be said. It is called 'tabernacle,' as if we were speaking of the tavern of God (*taberna Dei*), as will be explained in discussing the chapter *The Dedication of the Church*. In the chapter *The Altar*, we shall show why it was also called the 'tabernacle' or the 'ark of witness.' Then a church may take the name of 'martyrium' when it is built in honour of a martyr. The name of 'chapel,' *capella*, may also be used, as will be said in Book Two, in the chapter *The Priest*. Sometimes a convent (*coenobium*), sometimes a sacrifice, (*sacrificium*), sometimes a sanctuary,

---

[48] The Church Militant is the Church in this world while the Church Triumphant is the Church in Heaven

[49] Durandus is probable referring to the Greek word *dogma* which means 'decision' or ;decree'

(*sanctum*), sometimes a house of prayer, sometimes a monastery, (*monasterium*), and sometimes an oratory, (*oratorium*). Generally, however, any place established for prayer can be called an oratory. The Church is sometimes called the 'Body of Christ;' sometimes she is even called the 'Virgin,' according to this saying, 'I am jealous over you with godly jealousy: for I have espoused you to one husband, that I may present you as a chaste virgin to Christ.'[50] Sometimes she is said to be the 'bride' that Christ is betrothed to in the faith, for we read in the Gospel, 'He that hath the bride is the bridegroom.'[51] Sometimes she is called the 'mother' because every day she gives birth to God of spiritual sons in baptism. Again, she is at times called a 'daughter,' according to the words of the prophet, 'Instead of thy fathers shall be thy children.'[52] Likewise, she is called 'widow' sometimes, because of the afflictions which weigh upon her, she dresses in mourning and, like Rachel, she cannot console herself.[53] At times she is represented under the image of a courtesan (*meretrix*), because of the Church gathered among the nations, and because she does not close her bosom to any of those who return to her. Sometimes she is called City, because of the communion of saints, her citizens. Some have also said that she is garnished with walls, because of the rampart of the scriptures which it uses to repel the attacks of heretics. Lastly, a church is made of stones of different kinds, because the merits of each of its inhabitants are different, as will soon be said. Now all that the synagogue has received by the law, the Church now receives, with a large increase of grace, from Christ, whose bride she is. Surely the institution and plan of an oratory or a church are not new; for the Lord commanded Moses, on Mount Sinai, to make a tabernacle. It was to be made with marvellously woven and embroidered tapestries, and was divided by a veil into two parts, the first of which where the people sacrificed, was called the Sanctus or the holy place. The second was the interior, where the priests and the Levites

---

[50] 2 Corinthians 11:2
[51] John 3:29
[52] Psalm 45:16 The Vulgate has, 'Instead of thy fathers, sons are born to thee.' (Ps. 44:17)
[53] See Jeremiah 31:15

performed their duties, and this was called the Holy of Holies,[54] as will be said in the *Preface* to Book Four of this work.

5. Now after this tabernacle had been worn by the length of years, and somehow consumed with old age, the Lord commanded to make a temple which Solomon edified in a wonderful manner and work; and there were two parts as in the tabernacle.[55] It is from both, the tabernacle and the temple that our material church has taken its form. In its anterior part the people listen and pray, and in the sanctuary, the clergy pray, preach, sing, and administer the holy things.

6. Furthermore the tabernacle which was made during the journey of Israel represents the figure of the world which 'passeth away, and the lust thereof.'[56] It is also true that the four colours of the veils express how the world is composed of four elements. Therefore, God in the tabernacle is God in this world,[57] as in the temple red with the Blood of Christ. The tabernacle clearly offers the type of the Church Militant, which has 'no continuing city, but we seek one to come.'[58] That is why it is called tabernacle or tent, for tabernacles or tents belong to soldiers: and this saying, 'the Lord is in his holy temple,'[59] means, God is among the faithful collected together in His name. The outer part of the tabernacle, in which the people sacrificed, was the active life to which the people exercised themselves by the love of their neighbour. The other part, in which the Levites performed their service, is the contemplative life to which the pure and sincere souls of religious men are occupied with the love and contemplation of God; the tabernacle falls to make way for the temple because from battle one runs to victory and triumph.

7. Now, this is how one should build a church. After having prepared the place of the foundations, according to this saying, 'The house of the Lord is well founded on rock.'[60] the bishop, or the priest, who has obtained permission, must shed holy water

---

[54] See Exodus 26:33
[55] See 1 Kings 8:4-5
[56] 1 John 2:17
[57] See Psalm 11:4
[58] Hebrews 13:14
[59] Habakkuk 2:20
[60] See Matthew 7:24

there, to cast out the phantoms of demons from this place, and to place in the foundation the first stone, on which the sign of the cross will be engraved and made.

8. It must also be constructed in such a way that the head points straight towards the east; we shall speak of this in the *Preface* to Book Five. The head of the church will, therefore, be turned towards where the sun rises at the equinox, to signify that the Church, struggling on earth, must behave with moderation and equality of soul in joy as in afflictions; and do not turn the head towards the solstice rising, as some do. If, however, the walls of Jerusalem, which is built as a city,[61] are to be erected by the Jews according to the order of the Lord, as the prophet says, with how much more reason should we erect the walls of our church in the same way?

9. For the material church in which the people gather to praise God represents the holy Church which is built in the heavens of living stones, as we have already said. It is the house of the Lord constructed solemnly, whose foundation is Christ, who is the cornerstone;[62] the foundation on which was placed that of the Apostles and prophets, as it is written, 'His foundation is in the holy mountains.'[63] The walls built upon these foundations are the Jews and the Gentiles who have come to Christ from the four parts of the world, and who have believed or believe in Him. But the faithful, predestined to eternal life, are the stones employed in the structure of this wall, which will always be elevated and built up to the end of this world. Also, a stone is laid on a stone when those who teach in the church are zealously caring for children to instruct them, to take them back and strengthen them in faith. And in the holy Church, the one who brings relief to his brother in his sorrows is loaded with stones that he carries for the edifice of the spiritual house of God. Again, stones bigger than others, and those which are polished or united, which are placed outside the edifice, and between which the stones are smaller, represent men more perfect than the others, and who, by their merits and prayers, retain their weaker brothers in the holy Church.

---

[61] See Psalm 122:3
[62] See Ephesians 2:20
[63] Psalm 87:1

10. Now the cement, without which the wall cannot be durable and firm, is made of lime, sand, and water. Lime is the burning love which unites the sand, that is to say, undertakings for the temporal welfare of our brothers; because true charity takes care of the widow and the aged and the infant, and the infirm. This is why the faithful and those who have it study to work with their hands, so that they may be equipped to help others. Again, the lime and the earth, used to build the wall so that its stones do not collapse, are bound together by an admixture of water that is introduced into it. Without cement, the stones of the wall do not hold together and cannot constitute the solidity of the same wall. Now water is a symbol of the Spirit, so it can be understood that men cannot be joined together for the building of the wall of the heavenly Jerusalem without the love which the Holy Spirit produces in them. All the stones of the wall, polished and square, represent the saints, that is to say, the pure men who, by the hands of the Supreme Worker, are resolved to remain always in the Church. Among these men, some are carried and do not bear: they are the weakest and those who have the least experience in the Church, some are carried and bear, these are the spiritual stones of the middle of the wall and the mediators of their brothers to God. The others, and those who are perfect men, bear only and are borne only by Christ Himself, who is the sole foundation of the spiritual Church. And one love unites them all, as with one cement, till the living stones of the heavenly Zion become assembled by the bond of peace. Christ was our wall by His life and our rampart by His Passion.

11. Now, while the Jews were building the walls of Jerusalem, they had enemies against them who wanted to prevent their work, and they were so troubled by them, that with one hand they placed the stones on the wall, and with the other hand, they fought against the enemy.[64] So we also, who build the walls of the Church, are attacked by the enemies who have come from our womb and surround us; these are our vices or those perverse men who wish to prevent us from doing good. Therefore, in constructing the walls of the Church, that is, practicing the virtues of Christ, we must cast out enemies. Therefore according to the

---

[64] See Nehemiah 4:7

custom of the Jewish people and by their example, we must with one hand hold the sword of the word of God, and at last we shall clothe ourselves with the shield of faith, the breastplate of righteousness and the helmet of salvation.[65] So to defend ourselves against them with the help of the shepherd, or the priest who represents Christ in our midst, and who instructs us according to our duty and strengthens us by prayer.

12. Finally, the Lord showed Moses, in the Old Testament, what materials the tabernacle should be made of when He said to him, in Exodus, to take the firstfruits,[66] that is, all that is precious among the people of Israel; but receive it from him only who will offer it from himself and beyond what is necessary. Namely, 'gold, silver, brass, hyacinth, purple and scarlet twice dyed,' that is to say, cloths of hyacinth, purple, scarlet and bysse, which is a kind of flax of Egypt, supple and white. Also fleeces of goats and 'rams' skins dyed red,' which we call the fleeces and skins of Parcethia because the Parthians first thought of colouring them, 'and badgers' skins, and shittim wood.'[67]

13. Now 'Shittim' is the name of a mountain and a tree which is like the white thorn because of its leaves, and it is a very light wood which will not rot and which cannot burn. God added to this, 'Oil for the light, spices for anointing oil, and for sweet incense, Onyx stones, and stones to be set in the ephod, and in the breastplate. And let them make me a sanctuary; that I may dwell among them,'[68] so that they will not dread running to this mountain. Thus the expert master in the history of the Exodus continues.

14. Again the floor plan of the material church represents the form of the human body, for the chancel or the place where the altar is, represents the head, and both parts of the cross arms and hands; finally, the other part which extends to the west, the rest of the body. The sacrifice of the altar signifies the vows of the heart, and, according to Richard of St Victor,[69] the layout of the

---

[65] See Ephesians 6:14, 16, 17
[66] See Exodus 23:16
[67] Exodus 25:5
[68] Exodus 25:6-8
[69] Richard of Saint Victor was a Medieval Scottish philosopher, mystical theologian and one of the most influential religious thinkers of his time. He

church signifies the triple state of those who are to be saved in the Church: the order of virgins, the continents and the married.[70] The sanctuary is narrower than the chancel, and the chancel than the body of the church,[71] because the virgins are fewer in number than the continents, which are fewer in number than the married. Hence the place of the sanctuary is holier than the choir, and the choir than that of the body of the church, or the nave, because the order of the virgins is more just and holier than that of the continents, and the continents more than the married.

15. Besides this, the church stands on four walls, that is to say, it rises by the doctrine of the four Evangelists. It is long, broad, and rises above, that is to say, to the highest virtues. Its length means long-suffering, which patiently endures adversities, until it reaches the heavenly country. Its breadth is love which, dilating and expanding the soul of men, cherishes its friends in God and its enemies for God. The height of the nave is the hope of the reward to come, which makes it despise the happiness and misfortune of this world, until it sees 'the goodness of the Lord in the land of the living.'[72]

16. Indeed in the temple of God grace is the foundation of faith, which consists in believing what one does not see. The roof represents the 'love that covers the multitude of sins.'[73] The door is the obedience of which the Lord says, 'if thou wilt enter into life, keep the commandments.'[74] The pavement is the humility which the Psalmist says, 'My soul cleaveth unto the dust.'[75]

17. The four lateral walls are the four main virtues of religion, namely, justice, strength, prudence and temperance. These virtues are also, in the Apocalypse, the four walls of the city of God.[76]

---

was prior of the famous Augustinian Abbey of Saint Victor in Paris from 1162 until his death in 1173
[70] Virgins, continents and the spouses represent different states of the spiritual life
[71] The nave is the main body of the church. The word *nave* comes from the Latin *navis* or *ship* and is an early Christian symbol which may also have been suggested by the inverted keel shape of the vaulting of a church
[72] Psalm 27:13
[73] See 1 Peter 4:8
[74] Matthew 19:17
[75] Psalm 119:25
[76] See Revelation 21:16

The windows express hospitality with joy, and mercy accompanied by benevolence. It is of this house that the Lord said, 'we will come unto him, and make our abode with him.'[77] Some churches are made in the form of a cross, to show that we must be crucified to the world or follow Christ crucified for us, according to this saying, 'If any man will come after me, let him deny himself, and take up his cross, and follow me.'[78] Some churches, even, are built in the form of a rotunda, and describe it as a circle; this means that the Church has expanded through the whole circle of the world. Thus we may quote this saying, 'and their words to the end of the world,'[79] or else, from the circle of this world we shall reach the circle of the crown of eternity.

18. The choir of clerics is the place where they meet to sing together, or where the multitude of people gather to witness the holy mysteries. The choir took its name from *chorea* (dance) or *corona* (crown). In the old days the clergy stood round the altars, in the form of a crown, and arranged in this way sang the psalms, in the same tone. However Flavianus and Theodorus established that they could sing or chant alternately,[80] having been instructed on this subject by Ignatius, who had been at first instructed by God. Thus the two choirs of the singers designate the angels and the spirits of the righteous who praise God with a mutual will and exhort each other to excellence. Some derive the word *choeur*, 'chorus,' from *concordia*, or rather the agreement which consists and exists in love, for one who does not have love cannot sing properly. And what this chorus signifies, and why the eldest and the highest in dignity sit in the least and in the lowest place, will be said in the Book Four, in the chapters *The Office or the Introit of the Mass*, and, *The Procession of Priest and Pontiff to the Altar*. And when a single cleric sings, it is called in Greek *monodia*,[81] and in Latin *tycinium*, and when two clerics sing together, it is called *bicinium*, and when the singers are in great number, their melody a unanimous chorus, *choeur*.

---

[77] John 14:23
[78] Matthew 16:24
[79] Psalm 19:4
[80] Antiphonal chant
[81] 'single'

19. The exedra, or apse, is a vaulted enclosure, which is a meeting place somewhat separated from a temple or a palace, because it is outside the walls, which it is attached to. It has the same name, *exhedra*,[82] in Greek, and represents the lay faithful who are attached to Christ and to the Church. The crypts or subterranean vaults which are found in certain churches are the hermits, who lead a more retired life than other men.

20. The porch of the church signifies Christ by whom the entrance to the heavenly Jerusalem opens for us; it is also called a *porticus*, 'portico,' or *porta*, 'gateway,' or that it is open to all as a port (a *portu*).

21. The towers of the church are the preachers and prelates of the Church which form its rampart and defend it. For this reason, the bridegroom says this to the bride in the Songs of Songs, 'Thy neck is like the tower of David builded for an armoury.'[83] The pinnacle or summit of the tower represents the life or soul of the prelate who tends to higher things.

22. The rooster, placed on the church, signifies the preachers, for the rooster watches over the dark night, divides the hours by his song, awakens those who sleep, and celebrates the approaching day; and when he awakens he excites himself to sing, beating his flanks with his wings. All these things are not without mystery; for in the night of this age those who sleep are the sons of that night, lying in their iniquities. The cock represents the preachers who preach aloud and awaken those who sleep, so that they reject the works of darkness, and they cry, 'Woe to those who are asleep! Arise, you who sleep!'[84] They announce the light to come when they preach the Day of Judgment and future glory; but, prudent, before they preach the practice of virtues to others, they awaken from their own sleep in sin and chastise their own bodies. The Apostle himself bears witness of this, when he says, 'I keep under my body, and bring it into subjection: lest that by any means, when I have preached to others, I myself should be a castaway.'[85] And just like the cock, the preachers turn against the wind, when

---

[82] *ex*, 'out of,' *hedra*, 'seat'
[83] Song of Songs 4:4
[84] Compare with Ephesians 5:14
[85] 1 Corinthians 9:27

they strongly resist those who revolt against God, taking them back and convincing them of their crimes, in case they are accused of having fled at the approach of the wolf. The iron rod on which the cock is perched represents the inflexible word of the preacher, and shows that he should not speak of the spirit of man, but from that of God, according to this saying, 'If any man speak, let him speak as the oracles of God, etc.'[86] Then, because this rod itself is placed above the cross or on the top of it means that the scriptures are consummated and confirmed. That is why the Lord says in His Passion, 'All is consummated.' and the name of Christ was written in an indelible way on the book of the new scriptures.

23. The dome, that is to say, the summit of the high and round temple on which the cross is placed, signifies by its round form what perfection and inviolability the Catholic faith ought to preach and practiced; for, those who do not keep themselves whole and spotless, will die forever in eternity.

24. The windows of the church, which are made of transparent glass, are the divine scriptures which repel wind and rain and so prevent from entering into the church what might harm the edifice and the faithful gathered there. Also, while they give passage to the light of the true sun (which is God) into the church, that is to say, into the hearts of the faithful, they illuminate those who dwell in its bosom. They are wider within; because the mystical sense is more extended and surpasses the literal sense. The windows also represent the five senses of the body; their form means that they must be tightened outside, in order not to draw the vanities of this world into them, and are more open within to receive more widely and liberally the spiritual gifts.

25. The lattice in front of the windows represents to us the prophets and other obscure doctors of the Church Militant. Sometimes, to represent the two precepts of charity, two twin columns are placed on each side of the windows; they also remind us that the Apostles were sent out two by two to preach the Gospel to the nations.[87]

---

[86] 1 Peter 4:11
[87] See Luke 10:1

26. The door of the church is Christ and this is why we read in the Gospel, 'I am the door,'[88] says the Lord. The Apostles are also the doors of the church. The word *ostium* (door) comes from *obsistendo*, 'to stand facing those who are outside,' or *obsidendo*, 'to win, to take those who are out,' or *ostendendo*, 'to show them entry.' Also the swinging of the door, *valva*, comes from *volvendo*, 'to roll,' and 'portal' comes from *portando*, 'to carry,' because it is through it that one carries and brings into the church all that is offered to God.

27. The columns of the church are the bishops and the doctors who support the temple of God by the Catholic doctrine, as the Evangelists spiritually support the throne of God. And these, because of the resonating of the divine word of which they are the echoes, are called silver pillars, according to the words of the Song of Songs, 'He made the pillars thereof of silver.'[89] We also read that Moses placed five pillars at the entrance of the tabernacle and four in front of the oracle, that is to say, the Holy of Holies,[90] which will be explained in Book Six. Although there may be a large number of columns in the church, it is said that there are only seven, according to this saying, 'Wisdom hath builded her house, she hath hewn out her seven pillars,'[91] which means that the bishops must be filled with the grace of the seven gifts of the Holy Spirit, etc. 'James and John' (as the Apostle says) 'represent the pillars.'[92] The bases of the columns are the bishops, successors of the Apostles, who bear the whole weight of the church. The top of the columns represent the spirit of the bishops and the doctors. For just as members are led by the head, so our words are directed by our minds and works. The capitals are the words of the Holy Scripture which the Church tells us it is our duty to meditate on, and to which we are obliged to conform our actions, by observing them.

28. The pavement of the church is the foundation of our faith. Now, in the spiritual church, the pavement is the poor of Christ,

---

[88] John 10:9
[89] Song of Songs 3:10
[90] Exodus 26:32, 37
[91] Proverbs 9:1
[92] See Galatians 2:9

namely, the poor in spirit[93] who humble themselves in all things; therefore, because of their humility, they are assimilated to the pavement. The pavement which is trodden under foot also represents the people by whose work the Church is nourished and nurtured.

29. The beams which bind the walls of the edifice are the princes and preachers of the age, who defend and strengthen the unity of the Church, some by word, others by action.

30. The misericord[94] of the stall of the church represents the contemplatives in whose soul God rests without offence, and who, on account of their great merit, also contemplate beforehand the splendour of eternal life, and are compared with gold because of the splendour of their holiness. It is in this sense that one reads in the Canticles the following word, 'the bottom thereof of gold.'[95]

31. The framework of the church is the preachers who raise and support spiritually. The arches and their ribs are also the preachers, because they adorn and strengthen the house of God, and because the rottenness of vices must not reach their souls. It is from them that the bride boasts in the same Canticles, when she says, 'The beams of our house are cedar, and our rafters of fir.'[96] Indeed, God is building a church of living stones and incorruptible woods, according to this saying, 'King Solomon made himself a chariot of the wood of Lebanon.'[97] That is, Christ built His abode with the saints who were purified and had become incorruptible by chastity. We will discuss this later in the chapter *Pictures, Curtains, and Church Ornaments*. The sanctuary, that is to say, the head of the church, which is lower than the rest of the body of the church,[98] mystically signifies the great humility which the clergy or prelate ought to possess, according to the saying, 'The greater thou art, the more humble thyself in all things.'[99] The

---

[93] See Matthew 5:3
[94] A ledge projecting from the underside of a hinged seat in a choir stall which, when the seat is turned up, gives support to someone standing
[95] Song of Songs 3:10
[96] Song of Songs 1:17
[97] Song of Songs 3:9
[98] This is not common but can be found in a few churches
[99] Ecclesiasticus 3:20

balusters by which the altar is separated from the choir signify the separation which must exist between the things of the earth and those of heaven. In the chapter *Pictures, Curtains, and Church Ornaments* we shall speak of the sanctuary or the fence surrounding the choir.

32. The choir stalls, on which one sits in the choir, signifies that sometimes the body must be relaxed and the mind given recreation because work and ardour which are not alternated with rest are not sustainable.

33. The pulpit placed in the church is the life of perfect men and is thus called to signify, in a sense, a public desk, or located in a public place, and exposed to the eyes of all. In fact, we read in Chronicles that Solomon made a bronze scaffold, 'and had set it in the midst of the court: and upon it he stood, and kneeled down upon his knees before all the congregation of Israel, and spread forth his hands toward heaven.'[100] Ezra also made a wooden steps to speak from, and when he went up he was exalted above all the people.[101]

34. The name of *analogium* is also given to this desk. It comes from the Greek word *logos* because from it one reads and announces the word of God. It is also called *ambo*, from *ambiendo*, 'surroundings,'[102] because it surrounds, as it were, by a belt the one who ascends it. We shall speak of it in the Book Four, in the chapter *The Gospel*.

35. The clock, *horologium*, on which one reads and counts the hours *horoe leguntur*, signifies the eagerness and the care that the priests must have to say the Canonical Hours[103] at the required time, according to this saying, 'Seven times a day do I praise thee.'[104]

36. The tiles of the roof, which prevent the rain from penetrating into the sacred edifice, are the soldiers and knights who protect

---

[100] 2 Chronicles 6:13
[101] See Nehemiah 8:4
[102] This is a false derivation. *Ambo* comes from the Greek *ambon*, meaning 'step' or 'elevate.'
[103] Canonical hours mark the divisions of the day in terms of periods of fixed prayer at regular intervals
[104] Psalm 119:164

and defend the Church against the pagans and the attacks of the enemies of the faith.

37. The screw of the spiral staircase, built on the example of that of the temple of Solomon, is the path that crawls invisibly around the walls of the church, and through which we know, without being seen by anyone, the secret of all the mysteries of the spiritual edifice, the revelation of which belongs only to those who rise to heaven by meditating on its possessions. The steps by which one ascends to the altar will be spoken of in the following chapter.

38. The sacristy, where the sacred vases and ornaments are placed, and in which the priest clothes himself in the sacred vestments, represents the bosom of the most holy Virgin Mary, in which Christ has clothed Himself with the holy garment of His flesh. The priest on leaving the place where he has put on his vestments is advancing towards the people, because Christ, coming forth from the bosom of the Virgin, has come into the world. The seat of the bishop in the church is higher than that of the other priests, as will be said in Book Two, in the chapter *The Bishop*.

39. Near the altar, which again stands for Christ, is placed a pool or a basin, which shows the mercy of Christ, and we wash our hands in this vase to express that, in baptism and penance, represented by this, we are cleansed from the stain of sins. This was imitated from the Old Testament, for it is written in Exodus, that Moses made a basin of brass with its base, and placed it in the tabernacle, and that Aaron, the priest of the Lord, and the Levites, his sons, washed it before they came to the altar to offer incense.[105]

40. The light that is lit in the church is the figure of Christ, according to this saying, 'I am the light of the world,'[106] and John says, 'That was the true Light, which lighteth every man that cometh into the world.'[107] The lamps of the church signify the Apostles and the other doctors, by whose doctrine the church shines like the sun and the moon, and of whom the Lord has said,

---

[105] See Exodus 30:18-19
[106] John 8:12
[107] John 1:9

'You are the light of the world,'[108] for you give examples of good works. Therefore He warned them, 'Let your light so shine before men.'[109] Now it is according to the mandates of the Lord that the Church is enlightened. This is why in Exodus we read, 'thou shalt command the children of Israel, that they bring thee pure oil olive beaten for the light, to cause the lamp to burn always.'[110] This will be further discussed in Book Two, in the chapter *The Acolyte*. Moses also made seven lamps, which are the seven gifts of the Holy Spirit, which, in the night of this world, illuminate and dispel the darkness of our blindness. These lamps are placed on chandeliers, because 'the spirit of wisdom and understanding, the spirit of counsel and might, the spirit of knowledge and of the fear of the Lord,'[111] rested upon Christ, who, filled with His gifts, preached, to men captive in sin, the understanding of the liberty of the children of God.[112] The plurality of the lamps in the church designates the plurality of graces spread among the faithful and within their souls.

41. In many places the cross, the insignia of the triumph of Christ, is placed in the middle of the church, to express that we cherish our Redeemer from the depths of our heart, who, according to Solomon because of His extreme love, was 'paved with love, for the daughters of Jerusalem,'[113] and that all, seeing the standard of victory, say, 'Hail to you, the salvation of the whole universe, a beneficent tree;' and so that the love of God may never be forsaken by us, who, to redeem a slave, has given up His only Son, that we may imitate Christ crucified for us. Also the cross is placed in a high place to represent the victory of Christ. We shall speak of this in the chapter *The Dedication of the Church*. It will be explained in the chapter *Pictures, Curtains, and Church Ornaments* why the church is adorned within and not outside.

42. The cloister, as Sicard, the Bishop of Cremona says, originated from the place where the Levites were watching and sleeping, around the tabernacle, or in the forecourt of the priests, or the

---

[108] Matthew 5:14
[109] Matthew 5:16
[110] Exodus 27:20
[111] Isaiah 11:2
[112] See Isaiah 61:1
[113] Song of Songs 3:10

portico, which was before the temple of Solomon. For the Lord commanded Moses not to count the Levites when counting the multitude of the people, but to establish them on the tabernacle of the testimony, to carry it and to keep it.[114] It is because of this precept of the Lord that clerics must be separated from the laity in the church while they celebrate the holy mysteries. That is why the Council of Mainz ruled that this part, which is separated from the altar by balusters, would be reserved only for the chanting clerics. Finally, just as the temple represents the Church Triumphant, so the cloister is the figure of the heavenly paradise. In that place there is only one heart in fulfilling the love and will of God, where all will possess everything in common, because, what one will have less in himself, He will rejoice in having it in another; for 'God may be all for all.'[115] That is why the regulars,[116] who live together in the cloister, rise at night to go to the divine service, and, abandoning the good things of this world, put everything in common and live without having anything of their own.

43. The diversity of dwellings and offices in the cloister is the diversity of dwellings and rewards in the heavenly kingdom, for 'In my Father's house are many mansions,'[117] says the Lord. In the moral sense, the cloister represents the contemplation in which the soul retreats into itself, and where it hides after having separated itself from the crowd of carnal thoughts, and where it meditates only on heavenly things. In this cloister there are four walls, which are contempt for oneself, contempt for the world, love for neighbour and love for God. Each side has its row of columns, for the contempt of oneself is followed by the humiliation of the soul, the affliction of the flesh, humility in speech and similar things. The basis of all the columns is patience. In this cloister, the diversity of the dwellings is that of the virtues. The chapter is the secret of the heart, but we will speak of it in Book Five, in the chapter *Prime*. The refectory is the love of holy meditation. The cellar signifies Holy Scripture. The dormitory,

---

[114] See Numbers 1:47
[115] 1 Corinthians 15:28
[116] Members of a religious order subject to a rule of life
[117] John 14:2

pure consciousness. The oratory, the spotless life. The garden, planted with trees and grasses, represents the great number of virtues; the well of living waters, the abundance of gifts which quench thirst here below, and which in the future life will entirely extinguish its ardour.

44. As for the episcopal seats, which, according to the view of Blessed Peter, have been consecrated since the earliest times in every town, as will be said in the *Preface* to Book Two. The devotions of the elders dedicated them not to the memory of the confessors, but to the honour of the Apostles and martyrs, and especially of the Blessed Virgin Mary.

45. Besides, this is why we meet in the church. It is in order to ask God for the forgiveness of our sins and to diligently apply ourselves to singing the praises of the Lord, as is said in the *Preface* to Book Five, and to hear the good or bad judgements of the Lord, and to learn to know God, and to eat there the body of the Lord.

46. In the assembly of the church women and men are separated from each other, and Bede[118] informs us that this practice has come from an ancient custom of the Hebrews. It is for this reason that Joseph and Mary lost the Divine Child because; one thought that the Child whom he did not see with him was with the other. The cause of this separation is, that if the flesh of man and woman were more closely united, their bodies would be inflamed with lust. That is why, when we are to weep in this place for our sins, it is necessary to avoid what can serve to feed them and not to think of the satisfactions of the flesh. Men are in the south, and women on the north or northeast, in order to show that the saints who are strongest in the faith must resist the greatest temptations of this world and that those who are weaker in faith must be exposed to lesser or fewer attacks. Therefore the sex that is the strongest can be held in a place more unprotected and more exposed, because, according to the Apostle, 'God is faithful, who will not suffer you to be tempted above that ye are able.'[119] That also holds and relates to the vision of John who 'saw another

---

[118] c. 672–735, an English Benedictine monk whose writings are still highly regarded
[119] 1 Corinthians 10:13

mighty angel come down from heaven... and he set his right foot upon the sea,'[120] for the strongest members are opposed to the greatest perils. However, according to others men should be in the anterior part[121] and women in the posterior part, to express that 'the husband is the head of the wife,'[122] and therefore should go before her.[123]

47. The woman must also have a veiled head in the church[124] because she is not the image of God. It is through her that prevarication began in the world, and that is why in the church, and out of respect for the priest (who is the vicar of Christ), she must stand before him as before her judge, because of the origin of the fault with which she is accused. She will have her head veiled, and not uncovered. It is also with the same respect that she is not permitted to speak in the church before the priest. However, in the old days, men and women, taking pride in their hair, came into the church and sat there bare-headed, full of vanity because of their hair, which was dishonourable.

48. What conversation and discourses should be held in the church? The Apostle teaches us when he says, 'Speaking to yourselves in psalms and hymns and spiritual songs.'[125] We see by this that one must abstain from superfluous words, as Chrysostom[126] says, 'When you enter the king's palace, compose your face and your bearing, for the angels of the Lord are present, and the house of God is full of spiritual virtues.' Indeed, the Lord said to Moses, and the angel to Joshua, 'put off thy shoes from off thy feet, for the place whereon thou standest is holy ground.'[127]

49. Finally, it should be noted that the church, consecrated to God, protects and defends those accused of murder when they take refuge in its bosom, so as not to lose their lives or their

---

[120] Revelation 10:1-2
[121] The front or east end.
[122] Ephesians 5:23
[123] This should not be lightly dismissed as it points to a profound mystery
[124] See 1 Corinthians 11:5
[125] Ephesians 5:19
[126] St John Chrysostom, (c. 349-407) early Church Father, biblical interpreter, and archbishop of Constantinople
[127] Exodus 3:5; see also Joshua 5:15

members if they have not committed the crime in the church or near it. For it is said that Joab fled into the tabernacle, and was killed there, though he embraced the corner of the altar.[128] An unconsecrated church, in which Divine Offices are celebrated, enjoys the same privilege.

50. But the Body of Christ does not protect either the criminals who receive it or those who seek refuge near it. The reason for this is because this privilege is granted to the Church and is not to be extended to other things because the Eucharist is the food only of the soul and not of the body, and this is why it saves and delivers the soul and not the body.

51 There are three accounts on which churches can be moved from one place to another. First, because of persecution. Second, because of the difficulty and distance of the place; for example, bad weather or climate. Thirdly, when they are disturbed by the neighbourhood of the wicked, who go so far as to unite against it. These changes take place, sometimes with the advice of the pope, and sometimes with that of the bishop. In the Book Five, it will be said why the sign of the cross is given when entering the church.

---

[128] 1 Kings 2:28

2 THE ALTAR

1. An altar is raised in the church for three reasons, as will be said when speaking of its dedication. However to begin with, we must know that Noah,[129] first, followed by Isaac,[130] Abraham,[131] and Jacob[132] erected and built altars, as we read. By this name, we understand nothing but erected stones on which the victims of the sacrifice were slaughtered and killed, and which were then burnt with a fire lit underneath them. Moses also made an altar of shittim wood,[133] and an altar of incense, which he clothed with very pure gold, as it is written in Exodus,[134] where the shape of the altar is described. Solomon also, as we read in the book of Kings,[135] made an altar of gold. Now it is from these ancient fathers that the altars of the moderns have derived their origin, and why they are raised with four faces. Some are of one stone, and the others are composed of several stones.

2. Now, *altaria* and *arae* are sometimes indifferently used to designate an altar; however, there is a difference between these two words. For *altare*, 'altar,' is like saying *alta res*, 'a high thing,' or *alta ara*, 'a high pyre,' on which the priests burned the incense. *Ara*, 'altar,' a sort of *area*, 'an area,' or flat surface; or else it is called *ab ardore*, 'heat of fire,' because the victims offered to God in sacrifice were burnt there.

---

[129] See Genesis 8:20
[130] See Genesis 26:25
[131] See Genesis 12:8
[132] See Genesis 33:20
[133] See Exodus 25:11; Exodus 27:6
[134] See Exodus 30:3
[135] See 1 Kings 6:20

3. Also note that in the scriptures we read that the altar had many parts, namely, the upper and lower; inner and outer. These parts themselves are double in their use and sense. The upper altar is God the Trinity, of which we read, 'Neither shalt thou go up by steps unto mine altar.'[136] Again it is the Church Triumphant of which it is said, 'then shall they offer bullocks upon thine altar.'[137] The lower altar is the Church Militant, of which one reads, 'if thou wilt make me an altar of stone, thou shalt not build it of hewn stone.'[138] The lower part of the altar is also the table of the temple, of which it is said that the feast days should be spent in holy meals, seated and pressed at my table near, 'the horns of the altar.'[139] Also in the book of Kings, it says that Solomon made an altar of gold.[140] The interior of the altar is purity of the heart, as we shall see below. It is also the faith we must have in the incarnation; and it is on this subject that this order of the Lord is read in Exodus, 'An altar of earth thou shalt make unto me.'[141] On the outside of the altar is the wood pile or the cross of the altar itself, that is, the altar of the holocaust on which the night sacrifice is burned. That is why it is said in the Canon[142] of the Mass, 'Command, Lord, that these things are carried on your sublime altar by the hands of your holy angel.' The exterior of the altar also represents the sacraments of the Church, as it is said, 'thine altars, O Lord of hosts,'[143] are my dwelling. Again the altar signifies the mortification of our senses, or our heart, in which the movements of the flesh are consumed by the ardour of the Holy Spirit.

4. Secondly, the altar also signifies the spiritual church; and its four corners, the four parts of the world over which the Church extends its empire. Thirdly, it is the image of Christ, without

---

[136] Exodus 20:26
[137] Psalm 51:19
[138] Exodus 20:25
[139] Psalm 118:27
[140] 1Kings 6:22
[141] Exodus 20:24
[142] Canon law is the system of laws and legal principles made and enforced by the hierarchical authorities of the Church. The word 'canon' refers to one of these laws
[143] Psalm 84:3

THE ALTAR

whom no gift can be offered in a pleasing manner to the Father. This is why the Church is accustomed to address her prayers to the Father through Christ. Fourthly, it is the figure of the body of the Lord, as we shall say in Book Six, in the chapter *Holy Friday, Good Friday or Parasceve*[144] or Good Friday. Fifth, it represents the table on which Christ drank and ate with his disciples.

5. Now, in Exodus[145] one reads of the declaration which was deposited in the Ark of the Testament or the Testimony, that is, the tablets on which the testimony was written., we can also say the testimonies of the Lord to His people. This was done to show that God had revived, through the writing of the tablets, the natural law engraved in the hearts of men. Then there was a golden urn full of manna to testify that God had given bread to the children of Israel, and Aaron's rod to show that all power comes from the Lord God.[146] Again, in Deuteronomy, of a sign of the pact by which the people had said, 'speak thou unto us all that the Lord our God shall speak unto thee; and we will hear it, and do it.'[147] Because of this, the ark was called the Ark of the Testimony or the Testament, and because of this the tabernacle was called the Tabernacle of the Testimony. Now a propitiatory or covering was made over the ark; we shall speak of it in the *Preface* to Book Four. It is in imitation of this that in some churches, like in the temple of Solomon, an ark or tabernacle is placed on the altar, in which the body of the Lord and the relics of the saints are deposited. This speaks of how the prophet continually shows us, in fifteen psalms, the degrees which the holy man has raised in his heart.[148] The Lord also commanded to make a candlestick with branches in one piece, and it was of beaten pure gold.[149] It is written in the book of Kings,[150] that in the Ark of the Covenant nothing but the two tables of stone which were placed there by Moses on Horeb: when the Lord

---

[144] The Friday before the Jewish Sabbath
[145] See Exodus 40:20
[146] See Hebrews 9:4
[147] Deuteronomy 5:27
[148] Psalms 120-134
[149] See Exodus 25:31
[150] See 1 Kings 8:9

made a treaty of covenant with the children of Israel, at the time when they came out of the land of Egypt.

6. It should be noted that in the time of Pope Sylvester,[151] Emperor Constantine[152] constructed the Lateran Basilica, in which he placed the Ark of the Testament, which Emperor Titus had taken from Jerusalem, and the golden candlestick with the seven lamps suspended from its branches. In this ark there were the following things, namely, the rings and the gilded staves, the tables of the Testimony and the rod of Aaron. Also manna, the golden urn, the seamless robe, the reed, the garment of John the Baptist, and the scissors with which the hair of John the Evangelist was shorn.

7. Now a man is certainly the temple of God if he possesses within himself an altar, a table, a candlestick, and the Ark of the Lord. For he must have an altar where he offers with a right soul and where he shares righteously. The altar is our heart, in which we must offer and sacrifice to God; and this is why the Lord commanded to offer the burnt-offerings on the altar[153] because it is from the heart that the burning works of the fire of charity must arise and go forth. The word 'holocaust' is derived from the Greek words *holos*[154] or 'whole' and *kausis* which means a 'burning', or the 'heat of a fire.' So 'holocaust,' in a way, means things set ablaze and burned. Therefore, we must offer sacrifices on this altar with purity and share the victims with justice. We sacrifice well, when we bring to perfection the good of which we understand well; but we do not share beneficently if we do not do good with discernment. For man often thinks of doing good, and he does evil; and often, on the one hand, he practices good, and on the other, he commits evil; and thus the same man edifies and overthrows. But we share well, while we do not attribute to ourselves, but to God alone, the good that we do.

8. It is also necessary that man should have a table to bear the loaves of the word of God. By 'the table' we hear 'the holy scriptures,' of which the Psalmist says, 'Thou preparest a table

---

[151] In office from 314-335
[152] Constantine the Great, also known as Constantine I, was a Roman Emperor who ruled between 306 and 337
[153] See Exodus 20:24
[154] Durandus has *olom*

THE ALTAR

before me in the presence of mine enemies.'[155] In other words, 'you have given me scripture against the temptations of the devil.' We must have this table, that is, a place it in our soul, where we may eat the loaves of the word of God. It is in speaking of the scarcity of this bread that Jeremiah said, 'the young children ask bread, and no man breaketh it unto them.'[156]

9. A man also needs a candlestick, so that he may shine by his good works. The candlestick which shines outwardly is the good work, the flame of which kindles the torch of others by a good example; as it is said, 'No man, when he hath lighted a candle, putteth it in a secret place, neither under a bushel, but on a candlestick.'[157] The lamp according to the word of the Lord is a good intention, for Christ says, 'The light of the body is the eye,'[158] and the eye represents intention. We must not, therefore, place the lamp under a bushel, but on the candlestick, because if we have a good intention, we must not hide it, but let our light shine in good works.

10. It is also necessary that man have an ark, *arca*, which is derived from *arcendo*, 'to repel and chase.'[159] So the ark can be called the discipline or the regular life by which we chase sins away from us. Now in the ark, there is the rod, the tablets and the manna, to show that in regular life there must be the rod of correction, to chastise the flesh,[160] and the tablets of love, to cherish God. On the tablets are written the Commandments that relate to the love of God; we must also find there the manna of the ineffable and first sweetness of God, that we may 'taste and see that the Lord is good: blessed is the man that trusteth in him,'[161] and according to this proverb of the judicious woman, 'She perceiveth that her

---

[155] Psalm 23:5
[156] Lamentations 4:4
[157] Luke 11:33
[158] Luke 11:34
[159] *Arcendo* also means 'constraining'
[160] Chastising the flesh is also known as mortification. There are a comparative few who inflict physical pain on their bodies as acts of mortification but chastising the flesh has a wider spiritual meaning. This is the disciplining of self to control and subdue the wide range of earthly desires, an excess of which can impede spiritual progress
[161] Psalm 34:8

merchandise is good: her candle goeth not out by night.'[162] So that we may be the temple of God, let us have an altar for our offerings in order not to appear in the presence of God with empty hands, according to the words of Ecclesiastes, 'Thou shalt not appear empty in the sight of the Lord.'[163] Let us also have a table for our renewal, so as not to faint along the way, like fasting men, according to this word of the Gospel, 'I will not send them away fasting, lest they faint in the way.'[164] We need a candlestick, which we shall possess by doing good and not living in idleness, according to the saying of Ecclesiastes, 'For idleness has taught much evil.'[165] Let us have an ark, not to be like the sons of Belial, that is, unruly and without a yoke; for discipline is necessary, according to the saying of the Psalm, 'Kiss the Son, lest he be angry, and ye perish from the way, when his wrath is kindled but a little.'[166] All these things shall be spoken of, and also the other adornments of the altar, in the next chapter.

11. One who entirely adorns his heart with true humility and other virtues edifies this altar of which we have spoken; which led St Gregory[167] to say, 'He who amasses the virtues without humility resembles him who, in a great wind, carries dust in his open hand.'

12. Therefore, by the altar, we must understand our heart, as we shall say when we treat of the consecration of the altar; and the heart is in the midst of the body as the altar is in the middle of the church. It is with regard to this altar that the Lord gives this order in Leviticus, 'The fire shall ever be burning upon the altar; it shall never go out.'[168] Fire is charity; the altar is a pure heart. Fire will always burn on the altar; because charity will always be ardent in our hearts. This is why Solomon says in the Song of Songs, 'Many waters cannot quench love, neither can the floods drown it,'[169] for it is always burning, and its flame is inextinguishable. You, then, should act according to the word of

---

[162] Proverbs 31:18
[163] Ecclesiasticus 35:6
[164] Matthew 15:32
[165] Ecclesiasticus 33:29
[166] Psalm 2:12
[167] Pope Gregory I
[168] Leviticus 6:13
[169] Song of Songs 8:7

THE ALTAR

the prophet by keeping the holy day in meetings and meals near the altar; for the memories, even the weakest ones, which you will have afterwards, will make all your life a feast day.

13. The Apostle, touching on this, tells us and shows us that the most excellent way to perfection is charity,[170] because it is above all virtues, and whoever possesses it has them all. It is, in short, what the Lord has said, and what He says is so short, that I say it here: Have charity, and do whatever you will for, 'On these two commandments hang all the law and the prophets.'[171] Also the altar of each soul is to be built out of the living stones, that is, the various and diverse virtues.

14. The white cloths which cover the altar represent the flesh or humanity of the Saviour. They are whitened with great pain and labour; so the flesh of Christ that came forth from the earth, that is to say, from Mary, came to be immortal, through a great many sufferings, to Resurrection, splendour and gladness. This flesh of Christ is the figure of the sacraments of the Church, of which it is said, 'How amiable are thy tabernacles, O Lord of hosts, etc.'[172]

15. The altar is also the mortification of ourselves, or our heart, in which the movements of the flesh are consumed by the ardour of the Holy Spirit. Secondly, the altar also signifies the spiritual church; and its four corners, the four parts of the world over which the Church extends its empire. Third, it is the image of Christ, without whom no gift can be offered in a pleasing way to the Father. This is why the Church is accustomed to address her prayers to the Father through Christ. Fourth, it is the figure of the body of the Lord, as will be said in Book Six, in the chapter *Holy Friday, Good Friday or Parasceve*. Fifth, it represents the table on which Christ drank and ate with his disciples.

16. Now, we read in Exodus that the declaration, that is to say, the tablets on which the Testimony was written, was placed in the Ark of the Testament or of the Testimony of the Lord to His people;[173] and this was done to show that God had revived, by the writing of the tablets, the natural engraved in the hearts of

---

[170] See 1 Corinthians 13:2-8
[171] Matthew 22:40
[172] Psalm 84:1
[173] See Exodus 40:20

men; and a golden urn full of manna was added[174] to testify that God gave bread from heaven to the children of Israel; and the rod of Aaron, to show that all power comes from the Lord God; and in Deuteronomy, as a sign of the covenant by which the people said, 'speak thou unto us all that the Lord our God shall speak unto thee; and we will hear it, and do it.'[175] It was because of this, the ark was called the Ark of the Testimony or Testament; and because of this, the tabernacle was called the Tabernacle of the Testimony. Now they made a mercy seat or cover on the Ark; we will speak of this in the *Preface* of Book Four. It is in imitation of this that in some churches an ark or a tabernacle is placed on the altar, as in the temple of Solomon; and the prophet continually shows us, in fifteen psalms, the degrees which the holy man has raised in his heart.

17. Jacob saw this ladder, the top of which touched the heavens.[176] By these steps are understood, in a convenient and clear manner, the degrees of the virtues by which one ascends to the altar, that is to say to Christ, according to the Psalmist's words, 'They go from strength to strength.'[177] Again, Job says, 'I would declare unto him the number of my steps.'[178] The stairs that go up to the altar signifies a man in his own heart. Then Exodus says, 'Neither shalt thou go up by steps unto mine altar, that thy nakedness be not discovered thereon.'[179] for perhaps the ancients did not yet make use of trousers! One reads in the Council of Toledo, 'If it happens that a cleric, because of the pain he will feel at the death of one of his brethren, robs an altar or a statue of its dress clothes, or girds them with a funeral garment or thorns, or extinguishes the lamps of the church, let him be put down!' However, if his church is unjustly stripped of its rights, he is permitted to do so because of his grief. According to some, it is also for this reason that on the day of the Passion of the Lord the altars are stripped because of sadness; this, however, is reproved today by the

---

[174] See Exodus 40:23, Exodus 16:33-34
[175] Deuteronomy 5:27
[176] Genesis 28:12
[177] Psalm 84:7 The Vulgate has 'they shall go from virtue to virtue.' (Ps. 83:8)
[178] Job 31:37
[179] Exodus 20:26

Council of Lyon. Finally, the altars raised after dreams, or, in a way, the false revelations of men, are utterly reprobated.

3 PICTURES, CURTAINS AND CHURCH ORNAMENTS

1. The paintings and ornaments which are in the churches are the readings and writings of the laity; which led St Gregory to say, 'It is one thing to adore paintings, another thing is to learn, through the history that this painting represents, what we must adore.' For what writing shows to those who read it, paintings teach the unlearned who look at them, because, without instruction, they see in them what they must follow and read it in these paintings, although they do not know the letters. Now the Chaldeans worshipped fire and forced others to do the same, burning all their idols. As for the Gentiles, they worship representations or images and idols, which the Saracens do not do, animated as they are by this saying 'Thou shalt not make unto thee any graven image, or any likeness of any thing that is in heaven above, or that is in the earth beneath, or that is in the water under the earth;'[180] and by other authorities who immediately follow the passage quoted above, and they strongly reiterate this article. However, we do not worship these images, and we do not call them gods, nor do we place in them the hope of our salvation, because that would be idolatry; but we adore them by recalling to ourselves the memory of the accomplished facts which they represent to us. Hence the following verses:

> *What time thou passest by the rood, bow humbly evermore;*
> *Yet not the rood, but Him which there was crucified, adore.*

And again:

---

[180] Exodus 20:4

PICTURES, CURTAINS AND CHURCH ORNAMENTS

That thing, which hath his being given, 'tis fond for God to own:
A form material, carved out by cunning hands, in stone.

The form is neither God nor man, which here thou dost behold:
He very God and Man, of whom thou by that form art told.[181]

2. The Greeks also use images, and they paint them, as they say, from the navel upwards, and not below, in order to deprive those who see them of every opportunity of imprudent and ridiculous thought.[182] They also make no carved image, because of what is written, 'Thou shalt not make unto thee any graven image.'[183] Similarly, it is said, 'Ye shall make you no idols nor graven image.'[184] and again, 'Lest ye corrupt yourselves, and make you a graven image.'[185] Also, 'Ye shall not make with me gods of silver, neither shall ye make unto you gods of gold.'[186] Also the Psalmist exclaims, 'Their idols are silver and gold, the work of men's hands.'[187] 'They that make them are like unto them; so is every one that trusteth in them.'[188] 'Confounded be all they that serve graven images, that boast themselves of idols.'[189] Moses also said to the people, Israel, 'lest thou lift up thine eyes unto heaven, and when thou seest the sun, and the moon, and the stars, even all the

---

[181] Some later editions of the Rationale add:
   For it is of God the image teaches you; but God it is not itself.
   Look, honour, and in your soul know what it represents.
[182] Durandus, who was not in a position to know Eastern as well as Western symbolism, seems to have been mistaken here on a peculiarity of iconography among the Greeks. The Oriental represent only the half-body God the Father and the Son, and sometimes the Blessed Virgin. These representations are often more than four feet in height, and equal in size to the holy personages or angels represented by them. It is a manner customary among the Greeks, in order to make clear how far there is between the holiness and the power of the Father, of the Son, or of the Blessed Virgin, his mother, and those of the other saints
[183] Exodus 20:4
[184] Leviticus 26:1
[185] Deuteronomy 4:16
[186] Exodus 20:23
[187] Psalm 115:4
[188] Psalm 115:8
[189] Psalm 97:7

host of heaven, shouldest be driven to worship them, and serve them, which the Lord thy God hath divided unto all nations under the whole heaven.'[190]

3. This, also, is why King Hezekiah broke the bronze serpent which Moses had set up, because this people, against the precept of the law, burned incense before it.[191]

4. We see, therefore, by these authorities and others like them, that the excessive use of representations is repudiated; for the Apostle says, 'we know that an idol is nothing in the world, and that there is none other God but one.'[192] Furthermore the simple and the weak could easily be led to idolatry by the too great and indiscreet use of paintings or sculptures. So we read in Wisdom, 'Therefore there shall be no respect had even to the idols of the Gentiles: because the creatures of God are turned to an abomination, and a temptation to the souls of men, and a snare to the feet of the unwise.'[193] However there is no blame to be found in using paintings moderately to represent the evil to be avoided and the good to be imitated. Therefore the Lord said to Ezekiel, 'Go in, and behold the wicked abominations that they do here.'[194] Then, having entered, he saw a whole painting of reptiles and animals, and abomination and all idolatry painted on the wall of the house of Israel. St Gregory, explaining and expounding this in his *Pastorale*, says, 'The representations of external things attract God into the interior of the soul; and, in a way, all that one thinks, on seeing manmade images, is painted in the heart. When this is so, it is no longer true to say that the object to which one reflects on with attention in one's heart is the fictitious image painted in our eyes.' The Lord also said to the same Ezekiel, 'take thee a tile, and lay it before thee, and pourtray upon it the city, even Jerusalem.'[195] The following words of the Gospel further informs what has been said, namely, that images are the books of the laity, as Christ says, 'They have Moses and the prophets; let them hear

---

[190] Deuteronomy 4:19
[191] See 2 Kings 18:4
[192] 1 Corinthians 8:4
[193] Wisdom 14:11
[194] Ezekiel 8:9
[195] Ezekiel 4:1

them.'[196] This will be further considered in a later book. The Agathensian Council prohibits the making of paintings in churches, and of painting on the walls what is honoured and adored. However St Gregory says that it is not permissible to remove the paintings under the pretext that they should not be worshipped, for it is seen that painting moves the mind more than writing. In fact, by painting, the accomplished fact is placed before the eyes, while by writing the thing arrived at is recalled to the memory, as it were, by hearsay, which moves the soul less. That is why in the church we do not show such great respect for books as for images and paintings.

5. Of the paintings or representations, some are above the church, like the cock or the eagle; others outside the church, namely: on the doors and on the facade of the temple, for example, the ox and the lion. Finally, others are within, like the bas-reliefs and the various kinds of sculptures and paintings that are made, or on the vestments, on the walls, or in the stained-glass windows. Some of these have been considered in the treatise on the Church; that they were taken and imitated from the tabernacle of Moses and from the temple or the time of Solomon. Now Moses wrote, but Solomon wrote and painted, and adorned the walls of the temple with carvings and paintings.

6. Also we must know that the image of the Saviour in the church is painted chiefly in three ways. These are the principal and the most suitable to depict Him, that is, either seated on a throne or suspended on the gallows of the Cross or somehow sitting in His mother's womb and resting on her knees. Now, because John the Baptist pointed to Christ, saying, 'Behold the Lamb of God,'[197] some represented Christ in the form of a lamb. However, as the shadow has passed away and because Christ is a real man, Pope Adrian says that we must paint Him in the form of a man. 'For it is not the Lamb of God that is to be represented principally on the Cross; but after having placed a man on it, there is nothing to prevent a lamb from being painted in the lower or posterior part, since He is the true lamb bearing the sins of the world.' It is in

---

[196] Luke 16:29
[197] John 1:29

these, and in other ways that the image of the Saviour is traced, because of the different meanings which each brings with it.

7. For, painted in the manger, His nativity is recalled; on the breast of His mother, we see His childhood; painted or carved on the Cross, His Passion; and sometimes the sun and the moon are placed near the Cross in eclipse, to indicate His patience. When He is painted rising on a stairway, it speaks of His Ascension; represented as sitting on a throne or on a high seat, it indicates His present majesty and the power He now possesses, as if He were saying, 'All power is given unto me in heaven and in earth,'[198] 'I saw also the Lord sitting upon a throne, etc.,'[199] that is to say, the Son of God reigning over the angels, according to this saying, 'thou that dwellest between the cherubims.'[200] Sometimes He is painted together with Moses and Aaron, Nabad and Abihu, namely, on the mountain, and under His feet there was a sort of sapphire foot-walk, the glory of which was that of a serene sky,[201] because, as St Luke says, 'then shall they see the Son of man coming in a cloud with power and great glory.'[202] This is why He is painted surrounded by angels who always serve Him and are always at His side. They are represented with six wings, after this passage from Isaiah, 'Above it stood the seraphims: each one had six wings; with twain he covered his face, and with twain he covered his feet, and with twain he did fly.'[203]

8. The angels are also represented in the flower of their age and in a tender youth; because they never age. Sometimes the archangel Michael is also painted, trampling a dragon underfoot, according to the words of John, in the Apocalypse, 'there was war in heaven: Michael and his angels fought against the dragon.'[204] This battle is the separation of angels, the perseverance and strengthening of the good, and the ruin of the bad; or it is in the present Church the persecution suffered by the faithful. Sometimes also twenty-four old men are represented around

---

[198] Matthew 28:18
[199] Isaiah 6:1
[200] Psalm 80:1
[201] See Exodus 24:9-10
[202] Luke 21:27
[203] Isaiah 6:2
[204] Revelation 12:7

God, according to the vision of the same John, 'clothed in white raiment; and they had on their heads crowns of gold.'[205] These old men represent the teachers of the Old and New Testaments, who are twelve for their faith in the Trinity, whom they announce and proclaim in the four parts of the world; and they are twenty-four because of the good works and the observances of the gospel. When they are given lamps in their hands, this represents the gifts of the Holy Spirit; and if a transparent sea is laid beneath their feet, it refers to baptism.

9. Sometimes four animals are also represented, according to the vision of Ezekiel and St John. The figure of the man and the lion is placed on the right, that of the ox on the left, and that of the eagle on top of the other four.[206] These are the four Evangelists They are painted with books at their feet because they have accomplished in their souls and works what they have taught by their words and their writings. The human figure belongs to Matthew; Mark has that of the lion. These two are placed at the right hand of the throne of God because the birth and Resurrection of Christ were a general joy for all. That is why one reads in the Psalms, 'joy cometh in the morning.'[207] Luke is the ox, because he began his book by speaking of the priest Zechariah, and treated more especially than the other Evangelists of the Passion and the sacrifice of Christ. For the ox is the animal proper to the sacrifices of the priests. They also compare St Luke to the ox because of its two horns; in fact, his book contains both Testaments; the ox has four hoofs on its feet, and the Gospel of Luke contains the sentences of the four Evangelists. Christ is also figured by the ox, who was slain for us as an ox; and He is placed on the left because the death of Christ was distressing for the Apostles. We shall speak of all this in Book Seven, in the chapter *The Evangelists*, and it will be considered there the way in which the blessed Mark is to be represented. John is the figure of an eagle because he takes his flight to the highest regions when he says, 'In the beginning was the Word.'[208] This also means Christ,

---

[205] Revelation 4:4
[206] See Ezekiel 1:10
[207] Psalm 30:5
[208] John 1:1

whose youth is 'renewed like the eagle's,'[209] because, risen from the dead, He ascends and enters heaven. Here the eagle is not represented beside the throne of God, but above it, because it symbolises the Ascension and proclaims the Word is in God. But it will be said in Book Seven, in the chapter *The Evangelists*, why each of the same animals had four faces and four wings, and how they can be painted; finally, all this will be treated more extensively there.

10. Sometimes also the Apostles, who were His witnesses to the ends of the earth, by their words and their works, were painted around the throne of God, or rather underneath it. They are painted with long hair, as the Nazarenes had, that is, the saints; for there is the law of the Nazarenes which says, 'All the days of the vow of his separation there shall no razor come upon his head.'[210] Sometimes they are represented as twelve sheep, because, they were put to death for the Lord, but the twelve tribes of Israel are sometimes also painted under the image of twelve sheep. Sometimes, however, sheep are painted in larger numbers, and sometimes fewer, around the throne of the majesty of God. However, in this case, they signify something else, according to the words of St Matthew, 'When the Son of man shall come in his glory, and all the holy angels with him, then shall he sit upon the throne of his glory… he shall set the sheep on his right hand, but the goats on the left.'[211] In Book Seven, in the chapters of their various feasts, it will be said how the Apostles Bartholomew and Andrew must be represented.

11. Also notice that the patriarchs and prophets are painted with scrolls in their hands, and some Apostles with books, and some others with scrolls. Undoubtedly this is because before the coming of Christ the faith was shown figuratively, and was enveloped in many obscurities within itself. It is to express this that the patriarchs and prophets are painted with rolls, by which, in a sense, is designated an imperfect knowledge; but as the Apostles have been perfectly instructed by Christ, that is why they can make use of the books by which perfect knowledge is

---

[209] Psalm 103:5
[210] Numbers 6:5
[211] Matthew 25:31, 33

PICTURES, CURTAINS AND CHURCH ORNAMENTS

appropriately designated. Now, as some of them have written what they have learned to make it serve the teaching of others, they are appropriately depicted, as doctors, with books in their hands, like Paul, Peter, James and Jude. The others, however, not having written anything stable or approved by the Church, are represented not with books but with scrolls as a sign of their preaching. So the Apostle said to the Ephesians, He 'gave some, Apostles; and some, prophets; and some, evangelists; and some, pastors and teachers,'[212] for the work of His ministry

12. Now sometimes the divine majesty is represented with a book closed in His hands, because 'no man was found worthy to open and to read the book,'[213] other than the Lion of the tribe of Judah. Then at times with an open book, so that everyone may read what is in it; for He is 'the light of the world,'[214] 'the way, the truth, the life,'[215] and holds the book of life.[216] It will be said in Book Seven, in the chapter *The Evangelists*, why Paul and Peter are represented, one to the right and one to the left of the Saviour.

13. John the Baptist is sometimes painted as a hermit.

14. The martyrs are represented with the instruments of their execution, like St Lawrence on the framework and St Stephen with stones. Sometimes they are painted with palms, which mark their victory, according to this saying, 'The righteous shall flourish like the palm tree,'[217] so that, as the palm flourishes, so his memory is preserved. That is why palmers, those who come from Jerusalem, carry palms in their hands. This is to show that they have served and fought for that King who was gloriously received in the earthly Jerusalem with palms, who afterwards, having in the same city fought against the devil, and conquered, entered the palace of heaven in triumph with His angels; where the righteous shall flourish like the palm, and shine like stars.

15. Confessors are represented with their attributes; the bishops with mitres, the abbots hooded, and sometimes with lilies which

---

[212] Ephesians 4:11
[213] Revelation 5:4-5
[214] John 8:12
[215] John 14:6
[216] See Revelation 3:5
[217] Psalm 92:12

designate chastity, doctors with books in their hands, and virgins (according to the Gospel) with lamps.[218]

16. We depict Paul with the book and the sword; with the book, because he is a doctor or because of his conversion; with the sword because he is a soldier of Christ. Hence these verses:

The sword is the zeal of Paul,
The book is the conversion of Saul.

17. Commonly images of the holy Fathers are painted on the walls of the church, sometimes on the back panels of the altar, sometimes on sacred vestments and in other different places, so that we may meditate perpetually, not indiscreetly or uselessly, on their holiness. This is why, in Exodus, it was commanded by the divine law, that on the breast of Aaron, the breastplate of judgement should be bound with strings:[219] so that unmanly thoughts should never take hold of the priest's heart, which should be girt by reason alone. On this breastplate also, according to Gregory, the names of the twelve patriarchs are commanded to be carefully inscribed.

18. Surely, always bearing on one's breast the names of the Fathers, is to constantly be meditating on the lives of the ancients. Then the priest walks irreproachably into life, when he ceaselessly considers the examples of the Fathers who have preceded him, and follows in their footsteps, and represses within his heart forbidden thoughts, in case he strays beyond the limits of reason.

19. We must also consider that Jesus is always painted crowned as if He said, 'Go forth, O ye daughters of Zion, and behold king Solomon with the crown wherewith his mother crowned him.'[220] For Christ was crowned in three ways. First, by His mother, with the crown of mercy, on the day of His conception; this crown is double, because of what He had by nature and what was given to Him, and that is why it is called a diadem, which means a double crown. Secondly, He was crowned by his stepmother[221] with the

---

[218] See Matthew 25:1
[219] See Exodus 28:22
[220] Song of Songs 3:11
[221] The Latin *noverca* found here is normally translated as 'stepmother' and can be understood in the sense of an evil stepmother as one would in fairy tales

crown of misery and suffering on the day of the Passion. Third, He was crowned by His Father with the crown of glory on the day of the Resurrection; hence this word, 'For thou hast...hast crowned him with glory and honour.'[222] Finally, He will be crowned by those of His house of the crown of power, on the day of the last revelation. For He will come with the elders and senators of the earth to judge the world in His righteousness and equity. Thus all the saints are portrayed crowned, as if the Lord said, 'Daughters of Jerusalem, come and see the witnesses[223] of God with the golden crowns of which the Lord has crowned them.' In the book of Wisdom, it is said, 'the just shall live for evermore: and their reward is with the Lord, and the care of them with the most High. Therefore shall they receive a kingdom of glory, and a crown of beauty at the hand of the Lord.'[224]

20. Now this crown which we speak of is painted in the form of a round shield because the saints of God enjoy divine protection. That is why they sing, full of joy, 'thou, Lord, wilt bless the righteous; with favour wilt thou compass him as with a shield.'[225] However yet the crown of Christ is distinguished from that of the saints by the figure of the cross, because it is by the standard of the cross that He has deserved for Himself the glorification of His flesh and for us the deliverance from captivity and the enjoyment of life. Therefore when representing a prelate or a saint during his lifetime, his crown does not have a round shape but is a square shield, to show that he produces the flowers of the four cardinal virtues, as we see in the legend of Blessed Gregory.

21. Sometimes, paradise is painted in the church, so that its sight invites one to love and to search for heavenly rewards; sometimes, too, hell is represented in order to divert men from

---

where she would represent a witch, and ogre or the devil. *Noverca* is related to the Latin word *novus* or 'new.' It is associated with the Old Armenian *nor*, 'new' which can be associated with being 'under a new dispensation.' From this we can get the understanding of Durandus implying Jesus being 'under the new dispensation' or control of 'a wicked stepmother,' namely those who persecuted Him

[222] Psalm 8:5
[223] Martyrs
[224] Wisdom 5:16-17
[225] Psalm 5:12

vices by the terror of torture. Sometimes flowers and trees are joined with their fruits, to represent the fruits of good works, which grow by the roots of virtues and rise on their stems.

22. Now, the variety of paintings in the church designates the variety of virtues, 'For to one is given by the Spirit the word of wisdom; to another the word of knowledge by the same Spirit; To another faith by the same Spirit; to another the gifts of healing by the same Spirit; To another the working of miracles; to another prophecy; to another discerning of spirits; to another divers kinds of tongues; to another the interpretation of tongues.'[226] Now the virtues are represented under the figure of a woman because they soften and nourish. The veins of the vault, which are also called panelling and adorn the house of the Lord, are the simplest and least instructed servants of Christ, who adorn the church not by their doctrine, but by their virtues alone. Then the bas-reliefs that are carved on the walls appear to come out and advance towards the person who looks at them. This is because, when the practice of the virtues becomes so habitual to the faithful that they appear to them innate in themselves, and, as they are all natural, they manage to practice their various operations without effort. We will say in Book Four, in the chapter *The Reverence after Reading the Epistle*, what we must do after the reading of the epistle and how we represent the synagogue. We will also say in Book Three, in the chapter *The Pallium*, how we adorn the Romans pontiff with the pallium and it will be said at the beginning of Book Eight, when speaking about the month, how one represents the year, the twelve heavenly signs[227] and the months. Again, as the painters desire, we represent various stories of the New as well as the Old Testament, for the painters and the poets have always had the same power to dare to do all that they have liked.

23. Finally, the ornaments of the church consist of three things, that is to say, in the ornaments of the nave, the choir and the altar. The ornaments of the nave consist of veils, carpets, and hangings of purple, silk, etc.. The ornaments of the choir are dorsals,[228] carpets laid on the pavement, and cushions. The dorsals are cloth

---

[226] 1 Corinthians 12:8-10
[227] Of the zodiac
[228] Hangings, usually of rich material, at the back of a throne, altar, etc.

hangings that are suspended in the choir, behind the backs of clerics. The carpets, or *tapeta substraforia* in Latin, are sheets that are put underfoot, a sort of foot carpet, and specially reserved for bishops, who must trample underfoot the things of this world. The cushions are sheets that are placed on the seats or benches that are in the choirs.

24. The ornaments of the altars are chests and shrines, hangings, phylacteries, candlesticks, crosses, gold fringes, banners, books, veils and curtains.

25. Also observe that the chest in which the consecrated hosts are preserved signifies the body of the glorious Virgins, of which the Psalmist said, 'Arise, O Lord, into thy rest; etc.'[229] Sometimes it was made of wood, sometimes of white ivory, sometimes of silver, sometimes of gold and sometimes of crystal. Now, according to its various qualities, it expresses the different graces of the Body of Christ. The same chest, when it contains consecrated or un-consecrated hosts, refers to human memory; for man must constantly recall the good things which he has received from God, the temporal ones (which are represented by the un-consecrated wafers), as much as the spiritual ones (represented by consecrated wafers). Which was also represented in the urn where God ordered the manna to be deposited, which, though temporal, nevertheless prefigured this spiritual sacrifice, which is the one we offer; and the Lord recommended that this urn be an eternal memory for future generations, as it is written in Exodus.[230] Now the chests placed on the altar, which is Christ, are the Apostles and the martyrs; the hangings and linen of the altar are the confessors, the virgins, and all the saints, of whom the Lord said to the prophet, 'Thou shalt put them on as a garment.' As was said in the previous chapter.

26. Now *phylatterium* is one thing, and *phylatteria* is another. A *phylatterium*[231] is a small sheet or strip of parchment on which the Ten Commandments of the law are written; the Pharisees were accustomed to wear it before them as a sign of piety. Hence it is said in the Gospel, 'they make broad their phylacteries, and

---

[229] Psalm 132:8
[230] See Exodus 16:33
[231] Known as *tefillin* in Judaism

enlarge the borders of their garments.'[232] The word is derived from the Greek *phulattein*, which is to guard or keep, and *thorax*, which is law.[233] However the *phylatteria* (or reliquary) is a small vase of silver or gold, or crystal or ivory, or other precious material, in which the ashes or relics of the saints are enclosed. For when Vigilantius called the faithful *Cinericii*,[234] (because they preserved the ashes themselves), to testify contempt of his decision, it was ordered by the Church that they should be honourably preserved in precious little vases. This name is taken from the Greek *phulattein*, which is 'to preserve' and *termon*,[235] which means 'boundary' because in these vessels one keeps something from the extremity of the body of the saints, such as for example a tooth or a finger, or something similar. The tabernacle, mentioned in the chapter *The Altar*, is also placed on the altar itself in certain churches.

27. At the extremities of the altar two candlesticks are placed, to signify the joy of the two peoples who rejoiced at the nativity of Christ. These candlesticks, in the middle of which is the cross, bear small lighted torches; for the angel said to the shepherds, 'I bring you good tidings of great joy, which shall be to all people. For unto you is born this day in the city of David a Saviour, which is Christ the Lord.'[236] This is the true Isaac, which explains the laughter of his mother.[237] The light of the candlestick is the faith of the people, for the prophet says to the Jewish people, 'Arise, shine;' enlighten Jerusalem, 'because thy light is come, and the glory of the Lord is risen upon thee.'[238] Also the Apostle said to the Gentile people, 'For ye were sometimes darkness, but now are ye light in the Lord.'[239] For at the birth and rising of Christ a new star appeared to the magi according to Balaam's prophecy, 'there

---

[232] Matthew 23:5
[233] An apparent error as the Greek *thorax* means 'breastplate' or 'armour over the chest'
[234] Grey
[235] Durandus has *teron*
[236] Luke 2:10-11
[237] Genesis 18:12
[238] Isaiah 60:1
[239] Ephesians 5:8

shall come a Star out of Jacob, and a Sceptre shall rise out of Israel.'[240] This was also spoken of in the chapter *The Altar.*

28. The snuffers and tongs for trimming the lamp are the divine words with which we cut under the letter of the law, and thus reveal the spirit that shines within it, according to this saying, 'ye shall eat old store, and bring forth the old because of the new.'[241] The vessels in which the wicks, once cut, are extinguished are the hearts of the faithful, who observe the law to the letter.

29. The tongs, whose twin teeth serve to stir up the flame of the lamp, are the preachers, who instruct us in the pages of both Testaments, and kindle the fire of charity in those whose morals are already similar and identical.

30. The *scuta*, which are cups of equal size at top and bottom, made for warming water, are the doctors who do not conceal the treasure contained in their hearts, but who derive new and ancient things from them. They also do not place the lamp under the bushel, but on the candlestick,[242] so that those in the house of the Lord may receive light and warmth upon them.

31. The cross must also be placed on the altar; and it is there that the crosier places it, to later raise it again. This raising marks how Simon the Cyrenean bore the Cross after taking it from Christ's shoulders. The cross is placed on the altar, in the midst of the two candlesticks, because Christ in the Church was the mediator between two peoples. For he is the cornerstone, 'who hath made both one,'[243] to whom the shepherds of Judea came, and the wise men of the east. This will be discussed in another way in the *Preface* to Book Four, in the chapter, *The Procession of Priest and Pontiff to the Altar.*

32. The front of the altar is also adorned with a golden fringe, according to the saying of Exodus, that an altar should be built, 'And thou shalt cast four rings of gold for it, and put them in the four corners thereof.'[244] The altar sometimes signifies the heart of man, in which the sacrifice of the true faith must be offered by contrition; and then the golden fringe signifies the thought of the

---

[240] Numbers 24:17
[241] Leviticus 26:10
[242] See Luke 11:33
[243] Ephesians 2:14
[244] Exodus 25:12

good work with which we ought to adorn our forehead so it may shine before others. Sometimes the altar signifies Christ, and then the fringe of gold appropriately represents the ornament of charity. For just as gold prevails over all metals, so charity is above all other virtues; so the Apostle says to the Corinthians, 'the greatest of these is charity.'[245] So we must decorate our youth in its flower with the golden fringe of charity in order to be ready to give up and lose our lives for Christ. The banners are also erected on the altar, in order to continually recall in the church the triumph of Christ, by which we hope, in our turn, to triumph over the enemy.

33. The book of the Gospel is also placed on the altar because the Gospel has Christ for its author and He Himself bears witness to it. In Book Three, in the chapter *The Vestments of the Old Law of the Old Testament*, it will be said that this book is adorned outside. Finally, the sacred vases and others, in the house of the Lord, originated from Moses and Solomon. These vases were in great number and of varied use in the Old Testament, as can be read in Exodus, and they had different meanings, which we will not treat of here for the sake of brevity.

34. Now, all things belonging to the ornament of the Church must be removed or covered during the season of Lent. According to some, this is from Passion Sunday because from that moment the divinity was hidden and veiled in Christ; for He abandoned Himself and allowed Himself to be caught and flogged like a man as if he had no longer the power of divinity in Him. That is why it is said in the gospel of that day, 'Jesus hid himself, and went out of the temple.'[246] Then the crosses are covered, which represent the power of His divinity. Others do this on the first Sunday of Lent because from this moment the Church begins to speak of the Passion. That is why, during this time, the cross must be covered when borne in the church. Now according to the custom of certain places, only two coverings or curtains are kept in the temple. One of these is placed around the choir, the other is suspended between the altar and the choir, so that whatever is in the Holy of Holies, as well as the sanctuary

---

[245] 1 Corinthians 13:13
[246] John 8:59

and the cross, are then veiled. This is to signify that the letter of the law, that is, its observance according to the flesh, or that in the Old Testament and before the Passion of Christ, of the holy Scriptures was veiled, hidden and obscure. Those who lived at that time always had a veil before their eyes, that is to say, an obscure knowledge. This veils also signifies that sword which was placed before the gate of paradise. This is in order to express that the carnal observances of the law, darkness and the sword were rejected and dispersed by the Passion of Christ; thus all the curtains and coverings which we have spoken of are removed on Easter. The Old Testament speaks of ruminating animals and split hoofs, like the oxen that plough, this means discerning the mysteries of the scriptures and understand them according to the spirit. That is why, during Lent, there are only a few priests who enter behind the veil which hides the sanctuary, because they have been given to know the mystery of the kingdom of God.[247]

35. In connection with this, it is to be observed that three kinds of coverings are placed in the church. These are the one which covers the holy things, the one which separates the sanctuary from the clergy, and the one which separates the clergy from the people. The first signifies the letter of our law. The second, our unworthiness, because we are unworthy and, moreover, impotent to penetrate with our eyes the things of heaven. The third is the restraint we have to put on our carnal pleasures. The first covering, that is to say, the curtains which are stretched from both sides of the altar, and which relates to the priest penetrates the mysteries, has been represented, as will be said in Book Four, in the chapter, *The Secret, or the Canon of the Mass*, comes from what is written in Exodus, that when 'Moses had done speaking with them, he put a vail on his face,'[248] because the sons of Israel could not stand the brightness of his face. Also, as the Apostle says, 'even unto this day, when Moses is read, the vail is upon their heart.'[249] The second veil, or curtain, is laid in front of the altar for the celebration of the Mass during Lent. Its origin and its figure are derived from the one suspended in the tabernacle,

---
[247] See Matthew 13:11
[248] Exodus 34:33
[249] 2 Corinthians 3:15

which separated the Holy of Holies from the holy place, as will be said in the *Preface* to Book Four. This veil concealed the ark from the people, and it was woven with admirable art and adorned with beautiful embroidery of various colours, and it split during the Passion of the Lord; and, in imitation of it, curtains are still woven in various very beautiful colours. Exodus, chapter 26 and 36, deals with the first veil of which we have spoken, and says how the curtains are to be made. The third veil originated from the *peribolus* or wall which, in the early Church, made its way around the choir, and rose only to the height of the window-rail, and this can still be seen in some churches. The reason why it was no higher was so that the people, seeing the clergy chant and sing, should follow their good example. Now, more generally, a veil is erected, or a wall is erected between the clergy and the people, so that they cannot see one another; as if, by this action, they were saying to the priest, 'Turn away mine eyes from beholding vanity, etc.'[250]

36. However on the day of the Parasceve, or Good Friday, all the veils of the church are removed. This is because, at the Passion of the Lord, the veil of the temple was torn, and it was through it that we were revealed to the comprehension of the spiritual king, which was hidden before our eyes, as has already been said above. It was then that the door of the heavenly kingdom was opened to us and that power was given to us, in order not to be overcome by the lusts of the flesh[251] unless we yield to it. However, the veil that separates the sanctuary from the clergy is drawn or removed at Vespers on every Saturday in Lent, so that when the Sunday service begins the clergy can look into the sanctuary, because Sunday recalls the memory of the Resurrection.

37. This is also done on these six Sundays because there is no age in which there has not been the joy of the eternal; but it is a figurative joy, which is concealed in heaven, and represented by this veil. This is why we do not fast on Sundays, because of the glory of the Resurrection of the Lord, which occurred on Sunday. Now the first Sunday after Easter means the joy our first parents

---

[250] Psalm 119:37
[251] This does not refer solely to carnal desire but also generally to the excessive desire for materialistic pleasures and pursuits

had in paradise before sin. The second is the joy that a few men had in Noah's ark, when all the others were drowned in the waters of the flood. The third represents the gladness of the sons of Israel, while the other peoples were afflicted by the famine that took place under Joseph. The fourth, which they experienced under Solomon, living in peace.[252] The fifth, the joy they had in returning from the captivity of Babylon. The sixth, that which the disciples felt from the Resurrection to the Ascension, while the Bridegroom was with them by his presence and His appearances.

38. On the festival also, where one reads the nine lessons of Lent, the veil is lifted or pulled aside, but this practice has not existed since the first institution of the Church because at that time no feast was solemnly celebrated during Lent. Regardless of which day of the week a feast fell on, it was commemorated on the following Saturday and Sunday, as is seen in the twenty-sixth Canon of Pope Martin, and in Burchard,[253] and all this because of the sadness of that time. Then, on the contrary, it became customary, for instance, that the feast of the nine lessons during Lent should be solemnly celebrated on the day that it fell, and that, however, one should fast on that day as usual.

39. On the feast days, curtains are hung in the churches as they provide decoration because visible ornaments move our soul towards the invisible. These curtains are sometimes dyed with various colours, as has been said before, so that, by the variety of these colours, one sees and knows that man, who is the temple of God, must be adorned with the variety and diversity of virtues. The white curtain represents the purity of life; the red, charity; the green, contemplation; the black, mortification of the flesh; and the grey, tribulation. Sometimes, on the white curtains, draperies of different colours are also placed, to express that our heart must be purged of vices, and that it must have within itself the curtains of virtues and the variety of colours of good works.

40. Now, on the Feast of the Nativity of the Lord, some churches do not hang any drapery in the church; whether they are plain or beautiful. Those who do not put any of them up do this to signify

---

[252] See 1 Kings 4:20
[253] Burchard of Worms (d. 1025) was the author of a Canon Law collection of twenty books. Canons are the laws which govern the Church

our shame; for although we have great joy that a Saviour is born to us, we ought not, however, to be without shame in thinking that our sin was so great, that it was necessary that the Son of God should make 'himself of no reputation' for us, and take upon Himself 'the form of a servant.'[254] That is why, on the day of His death, we make no solemnity accompanied by joy; but a very great fast, although we solemnly celebrate the death of the other saints, and permit ourselves to eat and drink more delicately, as will be said in Bok Six, when we speak of Parasceve or Good Friday. Certainly, we blush, because the Lord died for our sins; but the saints suffered, not for our sins, but for Christ. Those who hang plain draperies in the church represent by this the form of servant which the Lord has clothed Himself with for us, and the humble cloths which He was wrapped in on that day. Those who suspend beautiful draperies think of the joy which is felt at the birth of a King, and show how we must be to receive such a Guest.

41. In some churches, the altar is adorned with precious blankets on the solemnity of Easter, and curtains of three colours are hung: red, grey, and black, which designate three epochs. The first lesson and the responsory being finished, the black veil is removed, which signifies the time before the law. After the second lesson and the responsory, we remove the grey veil, which designates the time under the law. After the third lesson, we take off the red veil, which signifies the time of grace, in which, through the Passion of Christ, the entrance has been opened to us and to the Holy of Holies and eternal glory. The draperies and linen of the altar were spoken of in the chapter *The Altar*.

42. On high feasts, the treasures of the Church are displayed to the people, for three reasons. First, by a consideration of foresight, that is, so that it may be apparent why it is prudent that they are kept by the person who has been charged with this. Second, out of respect for solemnity. Thirdly, in memory of their offering, that is, in remembrance of those who first offered them to the Church. The church is decorated pleasantly on feast days within and not outside, which indicates in a mysterious manner that all its glory comes to it from within: although it is despicable externally, yet it shines in its soul which is the throne of God. To

---

[254] Philippians 2:7

her, therefore, is this word spoken, 'I am black, but comely, O ye daughters of Jerusalem, as the tents of Kedar, as the curtains of Solomon.'[255] And the Lord said through the mouth of the prophet, 'I have a goodly heritage.'[256] The prophet, considering this again, said, 'Lord, I have loved the habitation of thy house,'[257] which is spiritually adorned with faith, hope and charity. The material and spiritual church must be cleansed, and this will be discussed in Book Seven, in the chapter on Easter, and the fifth working day or Thursday of the Last Supper. In some churches, it is customary to hang two ostrich eggs, and other things of this kind, which excite admiration, and which are seldom seen, so that the people may be attracted to the church, and touched more by the sight of these objects.

43. For some also say that the ostrich, forgetful bird that it is, abandons its eggs in the sand.[258] At last, after having seen a certain stars, she remembers, returns to them and cheers them by her presence. Ostrich eggs are therefore suspended in the church to express that if a man, because of his sin, has been forsaken by God, he may be suddenly illuminated by a divine light, and remembers his faults. On seeing this brilliant light he repents and returns to Him, and he will be armed by the rays of that beneficent light of which it is also said in Luke that the Lord looked at Peter[259] instantly after he had denied Christ. These eggs are also suspended in the church so that in considering them each person thinks that man easily forgets God, unless he is enlightened by the star, that is, by the influential grace of the Holy Spirit, and is reminded to return to Him by the practice of good works.

44. Now, in the early Church, the holy sacrifice was offered in wooden vases and in ordinary garments; for in those times 'the chalices were of wood and the priests of gold;' but now it is the opposite. Pope Severinus[260] ordered the use of glass vases; but, because they were fragile, Pope Urban, with the Council of

---

[255] Song of Songs 1:5
[256] Psalm 16:6
[257] Psalm 26:8
[258] See Job 39:13
[259] See Luke 22:61
[260] In office for a period during 640

Reims,[261] ruled that silver or gold vessels should be used. Sometimes, however, because of the poverty of some churches, tin vases were used, because this metal does not rust. Wooden or copper vessels should not be used. The chalice, therefore, must not be glass, because of its fragility and the danger which one is in of shedding (or spilling) the Blood of Christ. Nor should it be of wood, for this is a porous and spongy material, and it would absorb the Blood of Our Lord. Nor brass, or copper, for the force of the poison produced by this metal would provoke illness.

45. Observe that the name of the chalice[262] has derived its origin from the Old and the New Testament, 'Babylon hath been a golden cups in the Lord's hand, that made all the earth drunken.'[263] David also, 'For in the hand of the Lord there is a cup, and the wine is red, etc.'[264] In the same gospel one reads, 'Are ye able to drink of the cup that I shall drink of?'[265] and again, 'he took the cup, and gave thanks.'[266] Further, the golden chalice

---

[261] In 1140

[262] The word 'chalice' is not found in the King James Version. It was originally a cup for drinking; in Latin *calix*. The chalice is the sacred vessel where the consecration of the wine is made in the sacrifice of the Mass and many are engraved with a symbol or quotation. For example, around the cup of a chalice once used in the Abbey of Saint-Josse-sur-Mer, there are two Latin verses which read:

> *With wine and water mixed with the blood of Christ;*
> *By such expenditure is salvation for every believer.*

and

> *Let water mixed with wine become the blood of Christ.*
> *Let every believer be saved after receiving them.*

This Abbey, near Calais in France, dates from the 7th century and was a well-known place of pilgrimage. It was closed in 1772 and later destroyed. In the near-by village church a shrine to the saint was opened in 1922 and still remains a famous place of pilgrimage

[263] Jeremiah 51:7

[264] Psalm 75:8 Durandus paraphrases this verse: 'The chalice in the house of the Lord is full of the sweetness of a wine pure and unmixed. I will take the chalice of salvation, and I will invoke the name of the Lord'

[265] Matthew 20:22

[266] Luke 22:17

signifies 'the treasures of wisdom'[267] hidden in Christ, that of silver, the purification of sin, and that of tin is the sign of sin and of punishment. This is because tin holds the middle between silver and lead, and although the flesh of Christ was not lead, that is, sinful, He was like the flesh subject to sin, although He was not silver, that is to say, liable for His faults, He was, however, liable for our faults, for He 'took our infirmities, and bare our sicknesses.'[268] The chalice and the paten are considered in the chapter *Consecrations and Unctions*.

46. Someone, due to a little understanding of religion, may say that the Lord commanded Moses to make all the vessels of the tabernacle, for all uses and all ceremonies, of brass, as it is written in Exodus.[269] Such a man is like Judah and the enemy of the woman who poured perfumes on the feet of Christ. If he also says that the precious vessels and other ornaments of this kind could be 'sold for much, and given to the poor;' he is like Judas and acts in a contrary way to the woman who brought the alabaster box of ointment.[270] To him we say in reply: It is not that God is better pleased with gold than brazen ornaments, but that when men offer to God that which they value, by their adoration they overcome avarice. Moreover, these things signify the mortal duties of piety which we owe to God and the future glory which awaits us in the other life. That is why, also, in the ancient law, the Lord commanded to make the superhumeral[271] of the priest of gold, hyacinth, purple, a beautiful scarlet, and other very fine twistings, in order to show what great variety of virtues the priest must shine with. God also ordained that the altar, the mercy seat, the candlestick, and the other vases and ornaments of the altar, should be made of gold and silver. In Exodus,[272] we read that God also commanded to make the tabernacle of various precious things, as has already been said in the chapter *The Church and its Parts*. Again, the high priest of the law made use of various other magnificent ornaments and garments, as will be said in Book

---

[267] Colossians 2:3
[268] Matthew 8:17, which refers to Isaiah 53:3-5
[269] Exodus 27:17-19
[270] Matthew 26:9
[271] An ecclesiastical vestment worn over the shoulders
[272] See Exodus 25:30-33

Three, in the chapter *The Vestments of the Old Law of the Old Testament*. We shall also speak of all this in the chapter *The Dedication of the Church*, almost at the beginning.

47. Now the Council of Orleans has forbidden the divine mysteries to be employed in the ornamentation of nuptials, so that they may not be profaned by contact with the wicked and the impure pomp of the age. This certainly shows that one should not make a chasuble from the coat of any person whatsoever, or cut off from the same garment to make it into another adornment destined for the celebration of the sacred mysteries.

48. Pope Stephen further ruled that no one should use the vestments of the Church for any purpose foreign to divine worship and that they should be touched only by holy men, lest the vengeance which struck Belshazzar king of Babylon,[273] does not come in turn on the transgressors of these orders.

49. Pope Clement has also established that neither the dead nor their coffin should be buried, wrapped, nor covered with the pall, that is to say, the linen of the altar, or with the cloth or napkin that covers the chalice, or with that with which the priest wipes his hands after consecration.

50. Also when the pall, that is to say, the corporals and the veils, which are the ornaments of the altar, as well as the curtains which surround the altar, are soiled, the deacons with the lower officers of the Church, wash them in the sacristy and not outside. Now to wash the veils that serve the altar, one will have a new basin but the palls, that is to say, the corporals, should be washed in another vessel. The veils of the doors or curtains, which are stretched out in churches, at feasts, and during Lent, will be whitened also in another vessel. It was decreed in the Council of Lerida that every church has to wash the corporals and the palls of the altar in vessels appropriated for this, and nothing else will be washed in them. The same Clement also spoke of the pall or the altar covering, the covering of the seat of the priest who, clothed in vestments, is accustomed to offer the sacrifice, the candlestick or the veil, that is to say, the drapery or curtain which hangs behind the altar. He said that when these things become consumed with old age they are to be burned, and their ashes thrown into the

---

[273] See Daniel 5

baptistery, or into the cement of the wall of the altar of the church, or in the narrow spaces of the pavements, where no one passes. And observe that this is done because the ornaments of the Church are blessed, as will be said in the chapter, *Consecrations and Unctions*.

4 THE BELLS

1. Bells are bronze vessels invented first in Nola, a district of Campania; this is why the largest are called *campanae*, and the smallest, *nolae*.

2. Now the bell is consecrated and rung, so that, by the resounding sounds which it renders, the faithful are animated together to seek the good things of the eternal and heavenly rewards, and that the devotion of faith grows in them. The bell is rung, so that the fruits of the earth, the souls, and the bodies of those who believe, are preserved and saved; that the armies of the enemies, and all the wiles of the enemy, should be discovered, and that they should be driven away; that storms, tempests, hurricanes, the impetuosity of the winds and the thunderbolt, are appeased and calmed, and the dangerous thunder and the breath of the north wind are suspended and arrested; and so that the spirits of the storms and the powers of the air see their empire broken. Finally, the bell is sounded so that those who hear this sound may take refuge in the bosom of their holy mother the Church, and prostrate themselves before the standard of the holy cross, in whose name, 'every knee should bow, of things in heaven, and things in earth, and things under the earth;'[274] all these are things that are said in the blessings of the bell.

3. It must be known that the bells, by the strong and brilliant sound by which the people assemble in the church to listen, and the clergy 'To shew forth thy lovingkindness in the morning, and thy faithfulness every night,'[275] represent the trumpets, by which,

---

[274] Philippians 2:10
[275] Psalm 92:2

in the old law, the people were summoned to sacrifice; and we shall speak of this in Book Six, in the chapter, *The Holy Day of Pentecost*. Now, just as the sentinels of the camps are kept awake by the trumpets, so the ministers of the churches defend themselves from sleep by the sound of bells, and, lastly, to watch all night against the snares of the devil. Now our bells or brass signals are more sonorous than the trumpets of the old law because then God was known born in Judea, while now His name is spread over all earth. Our bells are also harder and stronger, for they signify that the preaching of the New Testament will be more durable than the trumpets and sacrifices of the old law because they will last to the end of the world.

4. For the bells signify the preachers, who, like the bell, must call the faithful to the faith; which was typified by the commandment that the Lord gave to Moses to have a garment made for the high priest that had seventy-two bells, which sounded when the high priest entered the Holy of Holies.[276] Also, the cavity of the bell indicates the mouth of the preacher, according to the words of the Apostle, 'I am become as sounding brass, or a tinkling cymbal.'[277]

5. The hardness of the metal indicates the mental ability of the preacher, which makes the Lord say, 'I have made thy face strong against their faces.'[278] The flap or the iron which strikes the lower part of the bell on one side and then on the other producing sound is a figure of the tongue of the teacher who, adorned with knowledge, makes both the Old and the New Testament resound from the teachings that his word draws from it.

6. So the prelate, without knowing the art of how to preach, would be like the bell without a beating, according to St Gregory's words, 'If the priest is ignorant of preaching, what a powerful cry will he utter; a public crier without a voice, he is like a mute dog who cannot bark.' Also the beating of the bell indicates that the preacher must first strike at his own vices and, correcting them, then go back to those of others, in case, contrary to the doctrine of the Apostle who said, 'when I have preached to others, I myself

---

[276] See Exodus 28:33-35 Durandus speaks of seventy-two bells. As this number is not mentioned in the Bible it appears that he is pointing to another mystery
[277] 1 Corinthians 13:1
[278] Ezekiel 3:8

should be a castaway.'[279] For God says to the sinner, 'What hast thou to do to declare my statutes, or that thou shouldest take my covenant in thy mouth?'[280] Certainly, because, by the example of his actions, the preacher kindles most of the time, to the practice of good, those whom he cannot touch and move by the erudition of his word. The chain by which the leaf is attached to the vase of the bell is the moderation which tempers the tongue of the preacher and makes him follow in all things the inspiration of the heart by the authority of Holy Scripture.

7. The wood from which the bell is suspended signifies that of the Cross of the Lord, and this is why the bells are sometimes suspended in the highest part of the bell tower because the Cross was announced by the most ancient Fathers. The supports which tie or nail together the parts of this wood are the oracles of the prophets. The iron tie which joins and unites the bell to the wood marks charity, by which the preacher boasts of being nailed indissolubly to the Cross, saying, 'God forbid that I should glory, save in the cross of our Lord Jesus Christ.'[281] The plate or semicircle nailed to the wood of the bell, and by means of which the bell is set in motion, signifies the right and just soul of the preacher, who, attaching themselves to the divine commandments, inculcated them in the ears of the faithful, often repeating them to them.

8. The rope which hangs from the bell and serves to sound it is humility, that is, the life of the preacher. The rope also marks the measure and extent of our own life. Besides this, as the rope begins with wood from which the bell is suspended, which represents the Cross of the Lord, it also designates the sacred scripture, which descends in a straight line from the wood of the holy cross. Now, just as the rope itself is made of three other small strings, so the scripture is confined to the following three things, namely, history, allegory, and the moral sense. So the rope that comes down from the wood into the priest's hand is the scripture which flows from the mystery of the Cross in the mouth of the preacher. This is why the rope descends to the hands of the bell-ringer because the scripture must pass into the works of the

---

[279] 1 Corinthians 9:27
[280] Psalm 50:16
[281] Galatians 6:14

preacher, through the practice of the teachings it contains. The raising and lowering of the rope, when the bell is ringing, also indicates that the sacred scripture sometimes speaks of high things and sometimes of low things, or that the preacher sometimes says things elevated because of some of his hearers, and sometimes for the sake of others, descends very low.[282] Besides this, the priest draws the rope downward as he descends from contemplation to active life; but is himself drawn upwards, when, by the doctrine of scripture, he rises in the regions of contemplation. He also draws the rope downwards when he understands the scripture to the letter that kills; and it is taken upward when he explains it in the spiritual sense. Again, according to St Gregory, 'the priest is drawn down and raised upward, when he reflects in himself and measures the abasement in which he fell by sin and the elevation to which he succeeds by doing.' When the rope is drawn, the bell rings, the people gather together to hear the explanation of the sacred scripture, the preacher is heard, and the people are united in the unity of faith and charity. Therefore the priest, who acknowledges himself to be the debtor of the preaching, will not shirk the duty of setting the bells in motion, for the sons of Aaron were sounding trumpets. So he moves the rope, the one who calls by his ministry his brothers or the people together. The ring attached to the end of the rope, and by which, in most countries, the rope is drawn; is the crown of reward and final perseverance in the service of God; it is, finally, the divine scripture itself. Pope Sabinian[283] established that the hours of the day would be sounded by the churches.

9. Now observe, the bells are usually rung for the Divine Offices,[284] twelve times during the twelve hours of the day. That is to say, at Prime, the first hour of the day, once, and at the last hour also, because all comes from one God, and will always be the same, All in All. At Terce, they are sounded three times for the second, third and fourth hours, which are included in this part of the Office. In the same way, they are sounded three times at Sext, namely, the fifth, sixth, and seventh hours. Similarly at

---

[282] See Galatians 2:2
[283] In office from 604-606
[284] The Divine Offices are discussed in detail in Book 5

None, one also sounds them three times for the same reasons. However at Vespers, which is the ninth hour, one rings not only once, but a great many times, because in the time of grace the preaching of the Apostles has been multiplied. Similarly, in the night, in Matins, one often rings, because the preacher must always shout, 'Awake thou that sleepest, and arise from the dead.'[285]

10. In general, however, during the Night Offices they are sounded three times; first with the rattle (*squilla*), which represents Paul and his sharp preaching. The second ring is Barnabus, who was associated with him in the apostolate. The third shows that when the 'Jews rejected the Word of God and his word, the Apostles turned to the Gentiles' and instructed them in the faith of the Trinity by the teachings of the four Gospels, which means that in some churches one rings four more times.

11. Also notice that there are six kinds of bells which one rings in the church namely, the *squilla* or hand bell, the *cymbalum* or cymbal, the *nola*, the *nolula*, which is the little *nola* or double bell, the *signum* or large bell. It is with the hand bell that one gives the signal of the meal in the dining room or refectory. The cymbal resounds in the cloister, the *nola* in the choir, the *nolula* or double bell in the clock; the *campana* in the bell tower and the large bell in the tower. However, any of these may generally be called a bell. And the bells are designated by different names, because the preachers they represent are obliged and bound to many duties.

12. During the whole seventy days [286] in which the holy Quadragesima[287] is included, on midweek feast days the bells must not be sounded with a great volley, or from top to bottom. Rather they should be tinkled, that is to say, sounded simply at the hours of the day and at Matins. However, in well-regulated churches, one rings twice at Prime; first, to call the people; secondly, to begin the Office. Three times at Terce, according to the number of hours that this Office includes, as has been said before, that is, once to call the people, the next to assemble them in the church, the third to begin the Office. The same is done at the sixth and ninth hours, and the bells are rung in the same order

---

[285] Ephesians 5:14
[286] of Septuagesima
[287] Lent

as at Matins. However at Mass and Vespers, one rings with two bells only; and, in the smaller or lesser churches, they simply ring the bells, as has been said above; and this must also be observed on common days. Then on Sundays and solemn days, one rings with a great volley, as at other times. This is because the preachers, represented by the bells, are in greater abundance in the time of grace, and preach, 'in time and out of season,' so that in the feasts which pertain to grace, one rings the bells more loudly and they sound for longer, in order to awaken those who sleep and those who are drunk so that they do not sleep too much. It will be said in Book Five, in the chapter *The Night Offices*, what is meant by the bell, when one sings, *Te Deum laudamus*, 'We praise you, O God, etc.'

13. When someone dies, we must ring the bells so that the people, hearing this, pray for him. Now they ring twice for a woman because while on earth she found pain and contempt. For, first, she made man the enemy of God, and secondly, because she was not blessed in his posterity. But one rings three times for a man because the Trinity has been found in man. For, first, Adam was made of the earth, then Adam's wife; finally man was created from both, and so there is a trinity. Then if he is an ecclesiastic, they toll as many times as he has had orders. Finally, we must ring out loud with all the bells, so that the people know for whom it is necessary to pray. The bell must also be rung when we drive the body to the church, and when it is taken from the church to burial.

14. The bells are rung during the processions, so that the demons, who dread this sound, flee, as will be said in Book Four, in the chapter *The Procession of Priest and Pontiff to the Altar*. For they are seized with fear when they hear the trumpets of the Church Militant, that is, the bells, as every tyrant trembles when he hears in his kingdom the trumpets of some mighty king who is his particular enemy.

15. The reason why the Church, on seeing a storm approaching, rings the bells, is so that the demons, hearing the trumpets of the Eternal King, that is, the bells, flee away and do not cause the tempest to burst. It is also by the sound of the bell that the faithful should be warned and invited, because of the danger that threatens them, to apply themselves assiduously to prayer. Now

the bells are silent for three days before Easter, as it will be said in Book Six, in the chapter *The Same Thursday of Holy Week*. Again, at the time of an interdict[288] the bells are silent, for often because of the sin of those for whom they are responsible, the language of the preachers is frozen in their mouth, according to the words of the prophet, 'I will make thy tongue cleave to the roof of thy mouth…for they are a rebellious house.'[289] The Church also has organs of which we shall speak in Book Four, in the chapter *The Sanctus*.

---

[288] In Catholic Canon Law, an interdict is an ecclesiastical censure or ban
[289] Ezekiel 3:26

5 CEMETERIES AND OTHER SACRED AND RELIGIOUS PLACES

1. Now let us speak of the cemetery and other holy places consecrated by religion. Of holy places, some are dedicated to the needs of man, others are dedicated to prayer. The places devoted to the needs of man are traveller's inns, hospitals and pharmacies, old people's homes, orphanages, and homes for wounded soldiers. For the holy Fathers and religious princes have established places of this kind, in which the poor, strangers, pilgrims, old men, orphans and children at the breast, hermits, the infirm, the sick and the wounded would be received and cared for. It should be noted that the Greek word *geron* is the same as the Latin word *senex* which means 'old'. Now of the various places intended for prayer, some are sacred, others are holy, and others are consecrated by religion.

2. Sacred places are those which have been consecrated according to the ceremonies required by the hands of the pontiffs or bishops, and which have been sanctified by God. They are called by different names, as has been said before, in the chapter *The Church and its Parts*. Holy places are those of immunity and the privileges assigned to the servants and ministers of the Church. It is forbidden for anyone, under the threat of certain punishment, to dare try to violate them or their right and special privilege. These places include the porches of the churches, and in some cases the cloisters which are in the houses of canons or regulars,[290]

---

[290] Here 'canons' implies priests 'regulars' refers to other members of religious orders, in both cases those living in community under a rule (*regula* in Latin), and sharing their property in common

in which all men are guilty of any crime whatsoever, fleeing the pursuit of justice, take refuge, and this takes place under the orders of the king.

3. The places consecrated by religion are those where the whole corpse of a man or just his head is buried, because no one can have two burials. The body or some other member, put in the ground without the head, does not constitute a place consecrated by religion. According to the law, the corpse of a Jew or a Gentile, or a child who is not yet baptized, makes the place where he was buried religious. Nevertheless, according to the Christian religion and the canonical doctrine, only a Christian corpse makes and constitutes the place religious. Note that all that is sacred is religious, and not the contrary. Moreover, a religious place can be referred to in various ways, namely a 'cemetery,' a *polyandrium* or an *andropolis*, which is the same thing. In the same way, a 'sepulchre' may also be called a 'mausoleum' or a 'dormitory,' 'mound,' 'monument,' 'prison,' 'sarcophagus,' 'pyramid,' 'tomb,' 'urn,' and a 'cavern' or a 'vault.'

4. *Cemetery*[291] takes its name from *cimen*, 'sweet,' and 'repose,' 'for there the bones of the dead repose sweetly, and await the Advent of the Saviour; or because in there are the *cimices*, that is to say, bugs of intolerable odour.

5. The Greek word *poluandron* (polyandrium) means, as it were, *pollutum antrum*, 'a filthy cave,' because of the bodies of the men buried there. For by *poluandron* we mean the multitude of men; for *polus*[292] means 'plurality,' and *andros* which is 'man'. According to this sense, it is the true name of the cemetery, because of the multitude of men buried there. It is also called 'the city of men,' which is the same thing.

6. The word *sepulchre* (*sepulchrum*) means, as it were, *sine pulsu*, 'without a pulse,' because the person placed there is deprived of a pulse, or else it is the place where bones are enclosed.

---

[291] The word 'cemetery' comes the Greek *koimeterion*, which means a 'sleeping place'
[292] Durandus has *tolu*

7. The *mausoleum*[293] was so called from a certain man whose name was Mausole, who was rich and powerful, and much loved by Artemis, his wife, so that after his death she built him a magnificent sepulchre which she called Mausoleum, named after her husband. It is from there that the custom of giving the name of 'mausoleum' to every magnificent sepulchre has been preserved.

8. The *dormitory* derives its name from *dormiendo*, 'to sleep,' because there the bodies of the saints who die in the Lord rest. *Tumulus*, or 'mound,' implies 'swollen earth,' because after a man has been put into the earth, one raises the soil a little bit above his remains to mark the place. A 'monument' is so called because the sight of it 'moves the soul,' *movet mentem*, of anyone who considers it, and makes them remember that we are ashes and that we will return to ashes. *Ergastulum*[294] or 'prison' comes from two Greek words, *ergon* which means 'a work,' or 'something produced' or from *ergasia* which is 'the work to,' 'the work of,' 'the labour,' 'gain' and *sterion* which is 'station,' 'or outpost'. There rest the bodies of those who die in the Lord; from which comes this saying, 'Blessed are the dead which die in the Lord.'[295]

9. The Greek word *sarkophagos*, 'sarcophagus,' comes from *sarx*[296] which means 'flesh,' and *phagein*, 'to eat,' because the flesh is eaten there, that is, consumed. 'Pyramid' comes from the Greek word *pur* or 'fire,' because bodies burnt by fire and reduced to ashes were preserved there. Alternatively, because, just as a fire begins wide and rises to a point, so also the pyramid fire is a sort of very high burial place. An example of this is found in Rome, in which the ashes of Julius Caesar were deposed; and the people corruptly call it the 'needle of St Peter,' while, however, it ought to be called 'Julia,' or 'Julius. Caesar caused a similar pyramid to be erected near Tours, near the shore of the Loire, and enclosed the ashes of a warrior, his friend, killed in a battle.

---

[293] The word derives from the Mausoleum at Halicarnassus (near modern-day Bodrum in Turkey), the grave of King Mausolus, the Persian satrap of Caria, whose large tomb was one of the Seven Wonders of the Ancient World

[294] An *ergastulum* (plural: *ergastula*) was a Roman building used to hold dangerous slaves in chains or to punish other slaves

[295] Revelation 14:13

[296] *sarkos* is the genitive form

10. Also *bustum*, 'tomb,' derived its name from what it contained; for 'busts,' (*busta*), or human bodies were buried in them. An *urna*, 'urn' is so named because in ancient times it was the custom to burn bodies on pyres and to keep the ashes assembled in urns of earth. The 'cave,' or 'vault,' is sometimes called 'double,' *duplex*, as will soon be explained.

11. It is said that the cemetery originated with Abraham, who bought a field near Ebron, in which was a double cavern where he was buried with Sarah and Isaac, Jacob, Adam and Eve. He bought it so that it might serve as burial for himself and his own. There was a double cave[297] in this place, because two people next to each other were buried there, both the husband and the wife, or in one the men and the other the women. Alternatively, this double cavern was made in the form of a chair in each of the sides of which all the members of a family were buried. This led Jerome to say that the three patriarchs were buried in the city of Ebron, and in a double cave, with their three wives. The upper part of the cave, which took the trunk above the kidneys, was called the first cave, and the lower part, which took the feet, the legs and the thighs, was called second cave.

12. Now, not everyone should be indiscriminately buried in the interior of the church; for it can be seen that it does not serve as a burial place, except for sacred burials. For Lucifer was cast from heaven and Adam thrown out of paradise; and what places are better for them than those they occupy, namely, hell for the demon and earth for a man? So also Joab was slain in the tabernacle, and Job triumphed over his dunghill. Moreover, we see from history that it is dangerous that an unworthy sinner should be buried in the church; as we read in a *Dialogue* of Blessed Gregory. He relates that a man sullied with debauchery had been buried in the church of the blessed Faustinus of Brescia and the same night Blessed Faustinus appeared to the guardian of this church, saying to him, 'Tell the bishop to throw out of the church the body which he has placed in this place, otherwise he will die within these thirty days.' However the guard was afraid to say this to the bishop, and the bishop died suddenly on the thirtieth day. In the same place we read of another man, who was buried in the

---

[297] See Genesis 23:9

church, and whose corpse was then found outside the church, although the shrouds had remained in their place. Also St Augustine says, 'Those on whom great sins weigh, if they are buried in sacred places, will have to be judged because of their presumption, because the sacred places do not deliver them, the fault of their temerity accuses them.' Therefore no body shall be buried in the church, or near the altar where the Body and Blood of the Lord are prepared and offered, unless they are the bodies of the holy Fathers are called patrons, that is, defenders; who, by their merits, defend their whole country. Also bishops, abbots, and priests worthy of the name, and the laity of a very great holiness. All others must be buried around the church, for example in the vestibule, or in the portico, or in the chapel, or beneath the vaults which belong to the church outside (the charnel-houses), or, finally, in the cemetery. This can be seen in the Canons *Præcipimus* and *Non oestimemus*. Now some say that a space of thirty feet in circumference around the church must be dedicated to the burial of the dead. Others say that only the circle around the church which the bishop made when consecrating the building is sufficient for this. 'To bury a man near the monuments erected in memory of the martyrs, it serves the dead in that, by the recommendation that one makes to the patronage of the martyrs, the affection that the holy witness of God will conceive for him, will increase the number of prayers and give strength to the supplications that will be addressed to God in his favour.'

13. In very ancient times it was customary to bury men in their own houses. However due to the stench of the corpses it was established that they would be buried outside the city. So a common place, sanctified by religion, was consecrated for this. The nobles, however, were buried on the mountains and in the middle, or at the foot of them, or at their houses. Besides, if anyone is killed in a siege, he cannot be put into the cemetery. Instead he should be buried wherever he may lie. If a merchant or a stranger dies on the sea, and land is near, he should be buried there, however if there is no nearby harbour he should be buried in some island nearby. If land is not in sight, a house should be made of planks, if they are available, and then this should be thrown into the sea.

14. Now, one should only bury a baptised Christian in a Christian cemetery, and not even all Christians. For example, a man killed in an act of mortal sin; or in adultery, or in theft, or some forbidden amusement. Laymen of a very great holiness must be placed in the cemetery. Therefore, where a dead man is found, he shall be buried because of the doubt regarding the cause of his death and if someone dies suddenly by playing the games in use, such as a ball game, he can be buried in the cemetery because he did not think of hurting anyone. However because he was occupied with the diversions of this world, some say that he must be buried without psalms and without the other ceremonies of the dead. If someone excites another to argue or fight and comes to die unrepentant, and without asking the priest for forgiveness, he should not be put into the cemetery. Some say that this should be so, given that the death was of his own hand; except in the case of his death resulting from defending his property. Nor, in the case of suicide, should one be buried in a cemetery, even if beforehand he was repentant and confessed his faults. On the other hand, if a man dies suddenly, not from some obvious cause but by the sole judgement of God, he may be buried in the cemetery. For the righteous man, at whatever hour he may come out of life, is saved, especially if, at the moment when the Lord took him, he was occupied with things which are permitted. The cemetery and the Office for the Dead are granted without obstacle to the defender of justice and the warrior killed in a war whose motive was according to equity. Yet they do not carry in the church those who have been slain, in case their blood defiles the pavement of the temple of God. Again if a man, returning from a house of prostitution or any place where he has fornicated, is killed on the way, or, stopping there for some cause, dies there, he shall not be buried in the common cemetery. This so if it can be proved that he has fornicated, and if it is not established that he confessed afterwards or has had contrition of his sin; otherwise he can be buried.

15. Again, a woman who dies in child-birth should not be brought into the church, as some say, in case the pavement become soiled by her blood. They say that her funeral should be outside of the church and she is then buried in the cemetery but this is not right, for then she would not deserve such punishment. It is therefore

permissible to carry her into the church, paying attention to the fact that the temple of the Lord is not defiled by any fluids from the body, and taking great care to prevent this.

16. However, a stillborn child, who was not baptized, will be buried outside the cemetery. Yet some say that they should be buried with the mother as being a part of her body.

17. Now the husband and wife must be placed in the same tomb, following the example of Abraham and Sarah, who did not choose a particular burial place. This is why Tobit [298] recommended to his son, when his mother had finished her days, that she should be buried in the same sepulchre with him. In the same way, every person must be buried in the tomb of his fathers, unless he has chosen his burial place to be elsewhere. Moreover, in the Council of Mayence a decree was made regarding those who are suspended from the communion of the faithful, that is to say those who, for their sins, suffer the greatest punishment. If they have confessed or desired to confess, and communicate, they may be buried in the cemeteries, and that offerings may be made and masses celebrated for them. In Book Seven, in the chapter *The Office for the Dead*, we will say how the body of man must be buried.

---

[298] See Tobit 14:12

6 THE DEDICATION OF THE CHURCH

1. As the church and the altar have been mentioned in the preceding chapters, it follows that we must add some details regarding their dedication or consecration. We will do this, first by saying where the consecration of the church originated. Then we will move on to considering by whom it is consecrated; then, finally, how we dedicate the church, and what the dedication itself signifies, and all the ceremonies which accompany it. We will speak about the Office of the Dedication of the Church in Book Seven. So we must first say where the dedication of the Church had its beginning. Regarding this, it should be remarked that Moses, following the precept of the Lord, made a temple, and consecrated it as well as its table and altar, also the vessels of brass and the utensils used to celebrate divine worship. Not only did he consecrate these things by the prayers which he addressed to God, but also, according to the command of the Lord, he anointed them with holy oil. It is also said that the Lord commanded Moses to make a holy oil[299] to anoint the tabernacle and the Ark of the Testament on the day of the Dedication.[300] In his turn, Solomon, the son of David, built, according to the command of the Lord, a temple with an altar and other things necessary for the perfect and entire celebration of divine worship, as can be seen in the book of Kings.[301] King Nebuchadnezzar summoned all of his *satraps* (the great of the kingdom) and the governors to the dedication of the golden statue he had had

---

[299] A chrism
[300] See Exodus 30:23-25
[301] See 1 Kings 6

THE DEDICATION OF THE CHURCH

himself made.[302] Therefore the Jews, as we read in Burchard, consecrated, by prayers addressed to God, the places in which they sacrificed to the Lord, and they did not make offerings to him except in the places that were dedicated to him. If, then, those who displayed such zeal in the shadow of the law acted like this, how much more should we, to whom the truth has been manifested, to whom 'grace and truth came by Jesus Christ,'[303] build temples to the Lord? We should decorate them as best we can, and consecrate them, according to the teaching of Pope Felix III, devoutly and solemnly by divine prayers and holy unctions, together with altars, vases, clothing and other objects necessary for the worship of God. It once happened in Baruth, Syria, that the Jews, having trodden a particular image of the crucifix, and having pierced its side, saw blood and water immediately come out of it. On seeing this the Jews were astonished and amazed; and having rubbed their sick with this blood, they were delivered from all their infirmities. As a result all of them, having embraced the faith of Christ, were baptised, and they converted their synagogues into churches, by consecrating them. From this, it became customary for churches to be consecrated, when previously only the altars were consecrated. The Church also established that, because of this miracle, the Passion of the Lord would be remembered on the fifth of the calends[304] of December. It was for the same reason that the church of this city was consecrated, in the honour of the Saviour, and in it a vessel containing some of the blood is preserved, and a solemn festival is celebrated on that day.

2. Secondly, it is to be noted that only the bishop can dedicate churches and altars because he is the image and figure of the Sovereign Pontiff, Christ, who spiritually dedicates the holy temple and without whom we cannot establish anything in the Church. That is why He Himself said, 'without me ye can do nothing.'[305] The Psalmist adds, 'Except the Lord build the house,

---

[302] See Daniel 3:2
[303] John 1:17
[304] The calends or kalends is the first day of every month in the Roman calendar. The English word Calendar is derived from this word. See Book 8 for further explanation
[305] John 15:5

they labour in vain that build it.'³⁰⁶ That is why the Council of Carthage forbids any priest from doing this, for this act cannot be done by someone of a rank lower than a bishop.

3. Now, as the holy Canons instruct us, the church, the altar, and other objects of this kind must not be dedicated, unless the Church has been endowed and provided with goods acquired lawfully. Without these conditions, it should not be deemed to be consecrated. In fact, it is stated that, as a bishop dedicated a church built from the product of usury and the violent seizure of property, he saw the devil behind the altar, seated in a pulpit, in pontifical vestments. The devil said to him, 'Consecrate this church; for it belongs to my jurisdiction since it is the result of usury and theft.' The bishop and clergy, full of terror, fled from there, and immediately the devil destroyed this edifice with a great crash.³⁰⁷

4. Similarly, the church that was built from a view of greed, and to which an inadequate dowry was assigned, like that in which a pagan or an infidel was buried, must not be consecrated. First, this corpse has been thrown out of it, and the church must be reconciled after the walls and woodwork have been scraped off. The same is true of an excommunicated person. If a pregnant woman has been buried in this place, the church may be consecrated without the body being thrown out, although its fruit is not baptized. Although some wise and learned men have written to the contrary, it may also be consecrated on Sundays and ordinary days, and several bishops may consecrate it. Several altars may be consecrated at the same time by the same bishop in a single church, even if another bishop with his priests is present.

5. Thirdly, we must say why one dedicates a church. This is done for five reasons. First, that the devil and his power may be entirely driven from this place. Therefore St Gregory reports in his *Dialogues* that a particular church, which had belonged to the Arians, had been consecrated and handed over to the faithful. As soon as the relics of St Sebastian and Blessed Agatha were brought there, the assembled people suddenly felt a pig running

---

³⁰⁶ Psalm 127:1
³⁰⁷ This sounds like symbolic folklore. What probably happened was that the bishop discovered that the endowment came from illegally acquired funds and therefore refused to consecrate the building

THE DEDICATION OF THE CHURCH

here and there between their feet. The pig, which could not be seen by anyone, soon rushed to the gates of the church and was gone; this filled the assembly with admiration and astonishment. The Lord was showing, so that it might be revealed to all, that the unclean inhabitants of this place must come out of it. For on the following night a loud noise was heard in the attic of this church, as if someone wandered in a confused state, fleeing across the roofs. Then on the second night, a louder sound rang out. Finally, on the third night, such a loud noise was heard, so that it seemed as if the whole church had been overthrown and undermined to its very foundations. Immediately the noise ceased, and from then on the ancient enemy no longer troubled the peace of this church. Secondly, so that those who seek refuge there may be saved, as can be read in the Canon of St Gregory. This is why Joab fled into the tabernacle and seized the horns of the altar. Thirdly, so that the prayers that are to be offered in this place may be answered. That is why it is said in prayer at the Mass, 'Grant that all who gather here to pray, in whatever tribulation they may be, receive the benefits of your consolations.' Solomon prayed at the dedication of the temple, as can be read in the book of Kings.[308] Fourthly, in order that praise is given to God, as he has been said in the chapter, *The Church and its Parts*. Fifthly, so that the sacraments of the Church may be administered. This is why the church itself is called a 'tabernacle,' as if it were the hotel of God (*taberna Dei*), in which the divine sacraments are enclosed and administered.

6. Fourthly, we must say how the church is consecrated. The bishop, standing with the clergy before the doors of the church, first blesses water into which he has put salt. While he does this inside the church, twelve candles burn before the twelve crosses painted on the walls of the church. Then the clergy, followed by the people, walk round the outside of the church and sprinkle holy water on the walls with a hyssop cluster. Arriving at each door of the church, the bishop strikes the lintel with his pastoral staff, saying, 'Lift up your heads, O ye gates; and be ye lift up, ye everlasting door; and the King of glory shall come in.' The deacon answers from within, 'Who is this King of glory?' The bishop

---

[308] See 1 Kings 8:30

replies, 'The strong and mighty Lord, the Lord mighty in battle.'[309] He repeats this and on the third time, when the door is opened, the bishop enters the church with a small number of his ministers, while the clergy and the people remain outside. The bishop then says. 'Peace to this house;' and then he says the litanies. Then, on the pavement of the church, a cross of ash and sand is made, in which the whole alphabet is written in Greek and Latin letters. Again the bishop blesses water, with salt, ashes, and wine, and consecrates the altar. Then he uses chrism to anoint the twelve crosses painted on the walls with chrism.

7. Certainly, all that is done here visibly, God, by an invisible virtue works in the soul, which is the temple of the true God, where faith establishes the foundation of the spiritual edifice. Faith lays the foundation stones, and charity consummates the work. The Catholic Church itself, which is composed of the assembly of a great number of living stones, is the Temple of God. For there are many temples in this world which form only one, whose only master is the true God, and whose foundation is true faith. Therefore, the dwelling that is to be dedicated is the soul that must be sanctified.

8. Now it is to be observed that consecration has two effects, for it appropriates the material church to the service of God, and represents our betrothal, that is to say, both that of the Church and of the faithful soul. For a house that is not consecrated is like a young girl destined for a man, but who is not endowed or joined to him in the union of the flesh by marriage. However when it is consecrated, it is given, and it passes into the hands of Jesus, as his only wife. Therefore any future violation is sacrilege. It also ceases to be the resort of demons as is clearly seen in the consecration of that temple, which was formerly called the *Pantheion*, Pantheon,[310] the temple of Rome consecrated to all the gods.

9. That is why we must speak first of the blessing of the water, concerning which the Lord says, 'Except a man be born of water and of the Spirit.'[311] For the water which is fit to wash bodies

---

[309] Psalm 24:7-8

[310] 'A place for all gods.' Durandus has *Panteon*. Consecrated by Pope Boniface IV

[311] John 3:5

deserves to receive from God such great virtue, that as it cleanses the bodies of their filthiness, so it purifies the souls of their sins. It is evident that this water, by the sprinkling of which the church is consecrated, signifies baptism, because in some way the church itself is baptized. Now, a church also designates that which is contained in its bosom, namely: the multitude of the faithful, from which it takes its name *ecclesia*, particularly since it encloses within its walls the assembly of the faithful; it is the container for the content.

10. Next, we must consider why salt is mixed with this water, since our Saviour, speaking of baptism, makes no mention of salt. He does not say, "If any man does not receive salt water, or water mixed with salt;" or something like that. What He says is, 'Except a man be born of water and of the Spirit, etc.' We may also ask the same thing concerning oil and chrism. It is to be noted that salt, in sacred scripture and according to the word of God, is often placed for wisdom, according to this words, 'Let your speech be alway with grace, seasoned with salt.'[312] Note also that the Lord said to His disciples, 'Have salt in yourselves, and have peace one with another.'[313] and again, 'Ye are the salt of the earth: but if the salt have lost his savour, wherewith shall it be salted?'[314] That is also why, according to the law, no sacrifice was offered without salt. It was used in every sacrifice, and we can, therefore, be persuaded by these examples that salt is used for wisdom. Wisdom is, indeed, the condiment of all virtues, as salt is the seasoning of all foods. It is for this reason that no one is baptized until he has tasted salt, even children, so that what they cannot have by practice, they have at least by the symbol or the meaning of the sacrament; and this is the reason why one does not bless water without salt. The second blessing of water will be considered in the following chapter.

11. Now the threefold interior and exterior sprinkling, with hyssop and holy water, represents the triple immersion observed in baptism; and it takes place for three reasons. First, to cast out demons; for holy water has the peculiar virtue of putting them to flight. That is why it is said about exorcising it, 'That the water

---
[312] Colossians 4:6
[313] Mark 9:50
[314] Matthew 5:13

may be exorcised, to put to flight all power of the enemy, and to exterminate the enemy himself, etc.' Secondly, to purify this church, and make atonement for sins committed in it: for all that is of the earth has been corrupted and defiled because of sin. This is also the reason why almost everything was purified with water under the reign of the law. Thirdly, to remove all curses and to bring in the blessing; for from the beginning, the earth was cursed with its fruit because it had been the fruit of disappointment. Water has not been subjected to any curse. From this it can be seen why the Lord ate fish, although it is not expressly said that He ate from the flesh of the paschal lamb, and this is because of the precept of the law, in order to give us the example of sometimes abstaining from what is permitted, and sometimes of eating it. The sprinkling around the outside of the church shows that the Lord who watches over His people sends His angel among those who fear Him.[315]

12. The three responsories that are sung during this time are the joy of the three orders of those who receive the faith, namely: Noah, Daniel, and Job. And it is because the grace of faith, hope and charity, are attached to this invocation that we sprinkle the base, the middle and the top of the wall. We shall soon speak of the interior sprinkling and will discuss the virtue of the hyssop in the next chapter.

13. The triple circuit that the bishop makes in sprinkling refers to the triple coming of Christ, for the sanctification of the Church. The first, when He came from heaven into the world; the second, when He descended from the earth into hell; the third, when He returned from hell and rose to heaven. These three circuits also show that the church is dedicated in honour of the Trinity. It also refers to the triple state of those who are to be saved in the Church, namely, virgins, continents and spouses; which is also the disposition of the material church, as has been said in the chapter *The Church and its Parts*.

14. Finally, the triple striking of the lintel of the door signifies the triple right which Christ has in His Church, because of which it must be open to Him. These rights are those of His incarnation, His redemption, and His promise of glorification. For the pontiff

---

[315] See Psalm 34:7

represents Christ, his rod His power. The three knocks at the door with the pastoral staff indicate the preaching of the gospel. But what is the crosier, if not the word of God, according to the saying of Isaiah, 'he shall smite the earth with the rod of his mouth, and with the breath of his lips shall he slay the wicked.'[316] Therefore, to strike the doors with the rod is to shake the ears of his flock by the voice of preaching. For the ears are the doors by which we bring into the hearts of our hearers the words of holy preaching; which makes the Psalmist say, 'Have mercy upon me, O Lord…That I may shew forth all thy praise in the gates of the daughter of Zion.'[317] What are the gates of the daughter of Zion, except the ears and the understanding of the faithful? Third, the three strikes with the rod and the opening of the doors signify that by the preaching of the pastors the unfaithful will come to the knowledge of the faith. Through it, the doors of righteousness open, and those who enter by them receive faith; therefore, the Psalmist says, 'Open to me the gates of righteousness: I will go into them, and I will praise the Lord: This gate of the Lord, into which the righteous shall enter.'[318] Therefore, the bishop knocks on the lintel, that is to say, he prays and speaks, saying, 'Lift up your heads, O ye gates; and be ye lift up, ye everlasting door; and the King of glory shall come in.'[319] That is, open the doors, strip away your ignorance and take it away from before your heart.

15. Now the question to the deacon, who is shut up in the church, is answered in the name of the people, 'Who is this King of glory?' is the lack of knowledge or the ignorance of the same ignorant people, who ought to enter.

16. The opening of the door is the ejection of sin. Therefore the bishop rightly strikes three times, because this number is well known and very holy; and in every dedication, the bishop must knock three times at the gates because there is no sacrament in the Church without the invocation of the Trinity.

17. And the triple proclamation, 'Open, gates, etc.,' signifies the threefold power of Christ, namely, that which He has in heaven, and over the world, and in hell. It is for this reason that the hymn

---

[316] Isaiah 11:4
[317] Psalm 9:14
[318] Psalm 118:19-20
[319] Psalm 24:7

of the Ascension says, 'Let the threefold machine of heaven, earth, and hell, lowered and subdued, now bend the knee.'

18. Now, the door having been opened, the bishop enters to mark that if he reasonably exercises his office, nothing can resist him, according to this saying: 'Lord, who will resist your power?' But he enters with only two or three so that all the words of consecration may remain in the mouth of two or three witnesses. Alternatively, because the Lord, having transfigured Himself in the presence of a small number of disciples, prayed for the Church, He said, 'Peace be to this house,'[320] and to all that dwell in it, for Christ, when He came into this world, made peace between God and man. For He came to reconcile us to God the Father.

19. After this, while the litanies are spoken, he prays prostrate on the ground, so that this house may be sanctified. For Christ also, having humbled himself before His Passion, prayed for all the disciples who believed in Him, saying, Father, 'Sanctify them through thy truth.'[321] After he has risen, he prays without greeting the people. He does not say, 'May the Lord be with you,' since in some way the church is not yet baptized, and because the catechumens are not only worthy of being greeted but also, although they are not yet sanctified, we must pray for them.

20. The clergy, who pray and sing litanies in the choir, represent the Apostles who interceded with God for the sanctification of the Church and of souls. The alphabet is written in the following manner on the pavement of the church. A cross of ashes and sand is spread across the church, and the alphabet is traced in the form of a cross, in Greek and Latin letters, (but not Hebrew, because the Jews have moved away from the faith), and they are written with the pastoral staff.

21. Now, the alphabet written on the cross represents three things: first, the cross-writing, composed of Greek and Latin letters, marks the union in faith of the two peoples, the Jews and the Gentiles, produced by the Cross of Christ. This is according to the saying that Jacob blessed his sons with crossed hands.[322] Now this cross, or the side crossing the church, that is, going

---

[320] Luke 10:5
[321] John 17:17
[322] See Genesis 48:13

from the left corner of the east to the right corner of the west, and the other from the right of the east to the left of the west, signifies that this people, who at first were on the right were now on the left, and that, from being at the head, they passed to the tail, and vice versa, by the power of the Cross. For Christ, coming from the east, left the Jews on His left, because they were unbelieving, and came to the Gentiles, to whom (though they had been in the west) He gave to be on His right. Finally, after having placed the Gentiles on the right, in the east, He visited the Jews on the left, in the west, for it is certain that they are more wretched than He had first found the Gentiles to be. This is why these letters are written obliquely and in the manner of a cross, and not straight because one cannot attain to this holy understanding who does not receive the mystery of the Cross and does not believe that he will be saved by the Passion of Christ. Wisdom will not enter into a badly disposed soul, and where Christ is not the foundation, one cannot build on it.[323]

22. Secondly, the writing of the alphabet represents both Testaments, because they have received their fulfilment by the Cross of Christ. For, in the Passion, the veil of the temple was torn because the scriptures were then opened and the Holy of Holies was revealed. That is what made Christ say when dying, 'It is finished.'[324] Now, all spiritual knowledge is contained in these few letters, and the cross is drawn transversely to express that one Testament is contained in the other, 'as it were a wheel in the middle of a wheel.'[325]

23. Thirdly, it represents the articles of faith. Now the pavement of the church is the foundation of our faith. The alphabet which is written there are the articles of faith, with which the ignorant and the neophytes of the two peoples are instructed, who are to be regarded as dust and ashes. According to what Abraham says. 'I have taken upon me to speak unto the Lord, which am but dust and ashes.'[326] So the writing of the alphabet on the pavement is the simple doctrine of faith in the heart of man.

---

[323] Durandus is clearly pointing to there being a deeper spiritual meaning to what he explains here
[324] John 19:30
[325] Ezekiel 1:16
[326] Genesis 18:27

24. The *sambuca*, or the staff with which the alphabet is written, signifies the doctrine of the Apostles or the mystery of the teachers by which the conversion of the Gentiles took place and the treachery of the Jews. Then, the bishop, approaching the altar, begins his prayer, while standing. He starts with these words, 'God, make speed to save us;' because he is now beginning the main part of the Office; and this versicle is recited, 'Glory be to the Father, and to the Son, and to the Holy Spirit.'

25. In spite of the fact that this blessing takes place to give glory to the Trinity, we do not, however, say 'alleluia,' as will be explained in the next chapter. Then the bishop consecrates the altar. Now, for this consecration, another water is blessed, as will be said in the following chapter. After the altar has been sprinkled seven times, the whole church is sprinkled three times inside, as has been done before for the exterior, without differentiating between the larger stones or smaller, because before God there is no acceptance of persons.[327] This is why we sprinkle the inside, to mark that the external ablution without the interior serves no purpose. It is also done three times, because, as has been said before, this sprinkling signifies the sprinkling and purification of baptism received by the benefit of the Trinity. This is done according to this saying, 'Go ye therefore, and teach all nations, baptizing them in the name of the Father, and of the Son, and of the Holy Ghost.'[328] Now, as the church cannot be immersed in water, as one immerses the one to be baptized, that is why it is sprinkled with water three times, replacing the triple immersion, so to speak.

26. The sprinkling is also carried on from the east to the west, and in the middle, once, in the form of a cross, because Christ ordered the whole of Judea and all nations to be baptized in the name of the Trinity. He also granted baptism its efficacy by the ministry of His Passion, beginning with the Jews from whom He had His birth. The rest of the water is spread at the foot of the altar, as will be said in the next chapter. There are, however, some who do not bless more water, but who use that which they blessed at the beginning for the whole course of the office. Meanwhile, the

---

[327] Or no differentiation between people
[328] Mark 28:19

choir sings this psalm 'Let God arise, let his enemies be scattered, etc.'[329] Also 'He that dwelleth, etc.'[330] In which there is mention of the church and of its consecration, as it is manifest by these words, 'God setteth the solitary in families.'[331] Then the bishop says, 'My house shall be called the house of prayer,'[332] because this Office is to make the church the house of God, and not that of the commerce of men.

27. Next, the twelve crosses painted on the walls of the church are anointed with the same chrism as the altar. These crosses are painted, first to frighten the demons, so that those of them who have been driven from there, seeing the sign of the cross, are filled with terror and do not have the presumption of returning to them. Secondly, as insignia of triumph; for the crosses are the standards of Christ and the signs of His triumph. They are therefore properly painted in the church, in order to show that this place is under the yoke of Christ the Lord.

28. For this is also observed in imperial pomp; and when a city submits to the emperor, he has his banner erected on its walls, so that it may float there. Also, it is to represent where it says that Jacob erected as a monument the stone which he had placed under his head,[333] that is, as a sign of glory, of remembrance and of triumph.

29. Thirdly, so that those who reflect on them should recall to their memory the Passion of Christ, by which He consecrated His Church on the day of His sufferings, as well as the faith which has descended since His Passion. This is why it is said in the Canticles, 'Set me as a seal upon thine heart, as a seal upon thine arm, etc.'[334] Now the twelve lights placed before these crosses signify the twelve Apostles who, by the faith of the Crucified One, have illumined the whole world, and whose doctrine has enlightened the darkness. Which led to St Bernard saying, 'All prophecy is true in the faith of the Crucified One.' Also the

---

[329] Psalm 68
[330] Psalm 91
[331] Psalm 68:5 The Vulgate has, 'God who maketh men of one manner to dwell in a house.' (Ps. 67:7)
[332] Matthew 21:13
[333] Genesis 28:18
[334] Song of Songs 8:6

Apostle, 'For I determined not to know any thing among you, save Jesus Christ, and him crucified.'[335] So, the painted crosses are illuminated on the four walls of the church, and anointed with chrism; because the Apostles, in preaching the mystery of the Cross, illuminated by the faith of the Passion of Christ in four corners of the world. They have inflamed many to the knowledge of Christ, anointed them with His love, and brought them to the brilliance of conscience, which is designated by oil, and by the smell of good fame, which is signified by balsam. Then, after having anointed the altar with chrism, the church is adorned; the lamps are lit, and Mass is said, for which the pontiff uses other vestments than those he wore during the sprinkling, as will be said in the following chapter.

30. Finally, it must be remarked that it is said that the church is consecrated by the blood of someone; this is why, according to Pelagius and Pope Nicholas, the Roman Church was consecrated by the martyrdom of the Apostles Peter and Paul. The church is consecrated, as has been said above, and the altars as will said in the next chapter, and the cemetery and other places, as has been said in the chapter *Consecrations and Unctions*.

31. Now it is said in the Old Testament that the temple was consecrated three times, first, in September; secondly, in March, under Darius; third, in December, under Judas Maccabee. However, after having been dedicated once, the church must not be re-consecrated, unless it has been profaned; which happens in three ways. Firstly, if it has been burnt in such a way that all its walls (or the greater part of its walls) have been destroyed. But if the roof only, or some of its parts, the walls remaining whole or at least slightly damaged, has been burnt, it must not be re-consecrated. Secondly, if the whole church, or the greater part, has fallen to the ground all at once, and has been repaired altogether or remade with other stones. This is because the consecration of the church consists above all in external conjunction, in the conjunction of stones, and in their disposition, as has been said in the chapter, *The Church and its Parts*. But if all the walls have fallen, not at the same time, but successively, and have been repaired, it is supposed to be the same church, and

---

[335] 1 Corinthians 2:2

therefore it must not be reconstructed. Instead, it is only exorcised with water and reconciled by the celebration of a solemn Mass, although certain wise and learned men wrote that it was necessary to re-consecrate it. Thirdly, the church must be re-consecrated if it is doubted that it was consecrated in the past, especially if there is no writing, painting, sculpture, nor witness who saw it or who heard about it, which (as some say) would be sufficient.

32. Similarly, the altar that has been consecrated once must not be rebuilt, unless it happens to be profaned. Such profanation happens, first, if the table, that is to say, the upper tablet on which the consecration takes place, has been disturbed or changed in its form, or, for example, broken at the middle into more than two large pieces. However, such a serious case must be, by right, referred to the judgement of the bishop. It is a very grave case if the whole structure of the altar has to be moved and repaired. The church, however, must not be re-consecrated because of the disturbance or fracture of the altar or its structure, because the construction of the altar is different from that of the church. If, on the contrary, the church is totally destroyed and the altar is not damaged, only the church will be rebuilt after it has been repaired, and the altar will not be rebuilt, although it is washed with exorcised water.

33. In spite of the fact that the main altar was consecrated, nevertheless, the other little ones must be consecrated, although some authors have said that it was enough that the consecration of the main altar of the church, to point out the others with the finger.

34. If the altar is slightly chipped at the edge, it must not re-build because of this. Secondly, the altar is reconstructed, if its seal, that is to say, the small stone with which the tomb or the cavity in which the relics are enclosed, has been disturbed or broken. This cavity is sometimes made at the foot of the altar, and sometimes there is no other seal because in this case, the first superimposed tablet holds the place of the seal, which it replaces. Sometimes this cavity is made in the rear of the altar, and sometimes in the front and within this cavity, as a testimony of consecration, it is customary to prudently enclose the letters of consecration written and signed by the bishop. These testimonies contain the name of

the bishop and those of his colleagues present at this ceremony, also the name of the saint in the honour of whom the altar is consecrated, as well as the church itself. When both the church and the altar are consecrated at the same time, one also adds the year and the day of the consecration. Thirdly, the altar is re-consecrated, if the junction of the seal to the cavity, or the table to the block of the altar, or another seal, has been broken. Also if any of the stones of the junction or the block, which touches either the table or the seal, is either disturbed or broken. The reason for this is that the consecration is most especially perceived in the conjunction of the seal and cavity, and of the table and block or inferior structure. For it is mainly in the conjunction of the seal, the cavity, the table and the foot of the altar or its lower structure that the consecration is intended and understood. Fourthly, we re-consecrate the altar if we have made such additions to it or to the conjunction of the table and the lower structure, to the extent that it loses it first form: for it is the form which constitutes the existence of a thing. However, it is not profaned by a small addition but then what is holy draws to itself what is not, provided, however, that the conjunction of the table and the lower structure is not greatly altered. Fifthly, the altar and the church are re-consecrated when there is doubt of their having been consecrated. Sixthly, with regards to portable altars, if the stone has been removed from the wood in which it was framed, and which somehow represents its seal, and has been replaced again in the same frame or in another, there are some who think that it must be re-consecrated. Others are of the opinion, that it is only necessary to reconcile it. Now although this altar is often transported from one place to another by order of the bishop and is carried on a journey (which is why it is called a portable or travelling), we do not reconcile it, nor do we reconcile it for that purpose in each of the places where it is carried.

35. If a consecrated chalice is gilded, must it be re-consecrated on account of this? For in doing this it would seem to be a new chalice since it appears new; one who renews the first aspect of a thing seems to have made a new vessel, and one who repairs an already established thing repeats it. Indeed, consecration attaches

to the surface of objects. That is why I said above that we had to rebuild a church whose monuments were decayed.

36. However, the contrary opinion is true, which holds that a church must not be re-consecrated, as I have said before, either because of the washing of the walls, or because of their painting, or else because of a small addition to them. For the same reason, if the shape of the chalice is not changed, and the vessel remains in its first state, why should it not be re-consecrated, just as the church should be repaired? It is because the church and the chalice are the same as before; therefore neither of them must be re-consecrated, as has been said above. But if the primitive form of the chalice is changed, it would be another matter, because it is the form of a thing which constitutes its existence, as I have said. However, if the chalice has been touched by soiled hands, (because profane and foreign matter is now attached to it), it is appropriate that the chalice is washed with exorcised water before the most holy blood of the Lord is sacrificed. But let us leave aside what has been said above concerning consecration, and let us say something about reconciliation.

37. In connection with this it must be remarked that the spiritual temple, which is man, is sometimes defiled. Both Leviticus 20 and Numbers 19 cite several actions that can lead to this. Also the prophet says, 'Purge me with hyssop, and I shall be clean.'[336]

38. The material temple, which is the church, is also defiled, according to the testimony of Pope Gregory and Leviticus.[337] Thus the prophet said, 'thy holy temple have they defiled, etc."[338] and the church is reconciled[339] in the same way as the temple, by washing it with water. Now the reconciliation takes place by the celebration of Mass, and the aspersion (sprinkling) of water solemnly blessed with wine, salt and ashes. Salt represents clear and distinct knowledge; the water, the people; the wine, the divinity; the ashes, the memory of the Passion of Christ. The wine mingled with water is the union of divinity and humanity in the person of the Son of God. Now, we mix these things together to

---

[336] Psalm 51:7
[337] See Leviticus 15:31
[338] Psalm 79:1
[339] Reconciliation is the technical term for the restoring a desecrated church to a state fit for the performance of the divine offices

show that the people, purified by the clear and distinct memory of the Passion of Christ, are united to Him. This ceremony is done by the bishop alone if the church is consecrated, and although he can also entrust this care to another bishop. That is to say the blessing of water and the reconciliation of the church, or only the blessing of the water, or even only reconciliation, if it has been blessed with water earlier. He cannot, however, entrust either of these ceremonies to a simple priest, unless he happens to assume this right by virtue of special privilege. If the church is not consecrated, it is immediately necessary, according to the constitution of Gregory IX, to wash it with exorcised water. There are certain authors who say that this washing can be done by a simple priest, on the order of the bishop, provided he has exorcised water for this purpose, which every priest must use. Nevertheless, some men of very great authority, when questioned on this subject, wrote that it was wisest on this occasion that this ceremony should be performed only by the bishop, without his being able to assign it to a priest. The reason for this is that the canons call for exorcised water, solemnly blessed with wine and ash, which is indeed true, but it must be looked at as an invariable rule only for a church dedicated to God. It is otherwise if the defilement has taken place in a simple oratory, which is neither a holy place nor consecrated by religion. Here each one makes and disposes of whatever he pleases as he wishes, and that this place is only for prayer, although perhaps the holy mysteries are celebrated there without the diocesan permission, and that the same place may be used for another purpose. The church must be reconciled in the following case.

39. If adultery has been committed inside a church it should be re-consecrated, etc.[340]

40. A church is also re-consecrated if a homicide has been committed in it, with or without bloodshed, but with intent in any way, and when there has been, in addition to the homicide, the shedding of human blood as the result of violence, or injury, whether of the nose or the mouth. For in the Old Testament[341] it was forbidden to shed blood or other bodily effusions in the

---

[340] The rest of this paragraph has been omitted as it is considered to be inappropriate for general publication

[341] See Leviticus 14, Leviticus 15

temple, and to prevent one who suffers such things from entering it. But if, without violence or insult, the blood flows in the church, from the nose, mouth, or in another natural way, or if, by chance, by play, or by a fortuitous event, it happens that such is scattered, this is acceptable. Again, if any animal is killed there, or even if someone dies there suddenly, or is killed by a stone, or by a falling beam, or by lightning; for these of course, and other similar things, we do not re-consecrate the church. Neither if a man, wounded outside, takes refuge in the church and dies there after losing much blood, because then the homicide did not occur in the church. But if, on the contrary, he is wounded in the church, then dies outside, or even if the blood has flowed from his wound only outside, it is something else. Even if the blood would not have flowed at all from his body in the church, for one looks only at the blows that produced the wounds. If the blood is spilt on the roof of the church, the building is not re-consecrated because this took place outside its walls.

41. If a theft or assault takes place in the church, it is re-consecrated according to the custom observed on such occasions. Similarly, as a result of all violence without bloodshed, it must also be re-consecrated, as certain authors assert. For example when the person who takes refuge in the church is forcibly drawn, or when he commits a break-in. Or even if, without bloodshed, a brawl has been engaged in it with tumult, bones broken and bruised, fleeing without his blood flowing, is severely beaten in the church, and condemned at this moment or at death, or at the mutilation, is drawn to be led to the place of execution. But as these cases are not expressed in the law, it is not necessary that the church is solemnly re-consecrated by the bishop. However, we believe that this would be appropriate, or that a priest, by order of the bishop, should wash it with exorcised water. It seems to me that we should say the same thing if the church has remained for a long time without a roof and without doors, full of litter and other refuse, destined for the accommodation of animals, or the natural wants of men, and that it has been indiscriminately open to the world as a place of retreat or an inn. It would perhaps not be so bad that in such a case it would be solemnly re-consecrated by the bishop. But suppose someone, after being murdered outside of the church, is soon after carried

into the church. If the man who killed him, or some other person, enters the church, and, believing him not to be dead, further assaults the wounded corpse from which blood flows, the church must be re-consecrated. This would be as much as a sign of horror and abomination, as for the violence and sin committed; although this man is no longer alive, yet his blood has been shed in this place by the violence of one of his fellow men. For violence, horror and insult are done to the corpse itself. But it is otherwise when, by honour and respect for the body of a man who has died naturally, his limbs are cut off or his entrails removed from him in the church, so that a part of it may be buried in one place and another one elsewhere.

42. A church is re-consecrated, in which a non-believer, or even a publicly excommunicated man, has been buried. In such a case the walls must be scraped. Now, in the cases mentioned above, which necessitate the reconciliation of the church following them, it is required that the need of this ceremony is at least based on a fact disclosed by common knowledge.

43. For scandal is the horror and abomination that one experiences because of the shame of sin and the violence committed in a holy place or in the church. In this place, where one asks for the forgiveness of sins, one who takes refuge in it must be in safety. In Leviticus[342] we read where as a saving sacrifice for sins flying bodies were liberated together with praises and this was also proposed, if the will is there, for the person who commits a mortal sin. However, it is not necessary for a person hidden there to be reconciled, because the church is the encounter with the sacred and it cannot defiled by this. Or rather the holiness of this place itself prevents its infamy. Some think to the contrary; that is to say, it must be reconciled, at least in secret, so as not to reveal the names of those who have sinned.

44. Reconciliation takes place for the example and warning to all, so that, seeing that the church, which has not sinned in any way, is washed and purified for the sins of another, they think how much they will have to suffer and work to correct their faults.

45. The cemetery also, in which a pagan, a non-believer, or an excommunicated person has been buried, must be re-

---

[342] See Leviticus 14:4-7

consecrated, after the cursed bones buried there have been thrown out of its enclosure, that is, if, they can be distinguished from those of the faithful. It is also re-consecrated in the cases enumerated above for the church. For the cemetery glories and rejoices in possessing the same privileges as the church, as will be said in the chapter, *Consecrations and Unctions*; for it is holy and sacred. It is re-consecrated by the bishop like the church, by the solemn sprinkling of water with wine and ashes which has been blessed.

46. It is noteworthy that in any part of the church or cemetery that violence or pollution has been committed, all other parts are deemed to be violated because of the interconnectedness between them. This has recently been partly softened by Pope Boniface; for although the consecrations of the church, the altar, and the cemetery are different, yet the immunity is the same for them all. This must not be restricted, however, only to one part of them or an individual part of them; which is true if the church and the cemetery are adjacent. For if one is distant from the other, one can be violated without the other. If therefore, one of them has been violated or polluted, the other has also been violated or polluted. For the same reason, if one of them is reconciled, both are also are deemed to be reconciled, because there is nothing so natural that everything is untied by the same cause that it has been bound, and that the right to chain and unleash is equal. Thus, if the cemetery has been violated or polluted, it is enough to reconcile the church. Some, however, assure, with simple reasoners of simplicity, that one cannot be violated in any way by the violation of the other, and that, therefore, each must be individually reconciled. However, the authority of the Pontifical is contrary to their opinion; for there is the particular form of the reconciliation of the cemetery. Finally, if the church or cemetery, or anything else is consecrated or blessed by an excommunicated bishop, these, some affirm, do not require reconciliation, since sacraments administered by such in the form of the Church are valid, as will be said in the, *Preface* to Book Three. But when, as has been said above, an excommunicated person or some excommunicated people profane the cemetery and the church, the following should be noted. The external sacraments and benedictions, which proceed from the hands and mouth of such

a person, appear as far as they relate to their own merits to be much more contaminated and to defile before God. Therefore, it is convenient to reconcile them before the faithful use these sacraments, as the text of the sacred Canons clearly teaches; for the Lord says through the mouth of his prophet, 'I will curse your blessings.'[343]

---

[343] Malachi 2:2

7 THE DEDICATION OF THE ALTAR

1. We consecrate only the church, but also the altar; and this is for three reasons. First, to offer sacrifices to God. For we read in Genesis, 'And Noah builded an altar unto the Lord; and took of every clean beast, and of every clean fowl, and offered burnt offerings on the altar.'[344] The sacrifice that we offer on this altar is the Body and Blood of Christ, immolated in memory of the Lord's Passion, according to this saying, 'this do in remembrance of me.'[345]

2. Second, to invoke the name of God. This is why it says that Abraham, 'builded an altar unto the Lord, and called upon the name of the Lord.'[346] Now, this invocation which takes place on the altar is properly called the Mass.

3. Thirdly, to sing, 'he gave him power against his enemies: And he set singers before the altar, and by their voices he made sweet melody.'[347]

4. Now, here is the manner and order for the consecration of the altar. First, the pontiff begins with these words, 'Lord, come to my aid.' Afterwards, he blesses the water; then he makes four crosses with holy water to the four horns of the altar. Then he goes around the altar seven times and sprinkles the altar table at the same time, with an aspersory of hyssop and with holy water. He also sprinkles the church and then spreads the rest of the water at the foot of the altar. Four crucifixes are then made with the chrism at the four corners of the sepulchre in which the relics

---

[344] Genesis 8:20
[345] Luke 22:19
[346] Genesis 12:8
[347] Ecclesiasticus 47:10-11

are to be enclosed, and they are placed in a small chest or a small coffer, with three grains of incense, and they are enclosed in this state in the sepulchre. Next, the cover is placed on this tomb with the sign of the cross which has been drawn in the middle. After that, the altar stone (called its table) is put in place; and when this is done, it is sprinkled with oil in five places, and then anointed with the chrism, in the same manner as was said for the oil. The altar is also confirmed on the front where the cross is marked with the chrism, and incense is burnt over it in five places. After that, the altar is covered with white cloths, and finally, the sacrifice of the Mass is celebrated. Now each of the things will be looked at in more detail.

5. First, then, it is to be remarked that the altar is consecrated by means of the anointing with the chrism and the blessing and that it is only of whole stone. Then the pontiff, standing up, begins with these words, 'O God, make speed to save us,' because the Lord Himself says, 'without me ye can do nothing.'[348]

6. Now as the dedication represents those who are to be baptized, and who, having received the faith, prepare themselves for battle, and are still in the midst of the sighs and skirmishes of this subject, that is why we do not say, 'alleluia.' For those who are not baptized do not deserve the praise of angels. Which comes from where it says, 'Alleluia shall be sung in its streets.'[349] However, after the consecration of the church or the altar has been accomplished, the alleluia is sung, because after the delusions of the demons have been expelled, God will be praised. For Christ, advancing towards the altar of the Cross, unleashed death to manifest the glory of His eternity; but He only sang, 'alleluia,' after His Resurrection.

7. Secondly, with regard to the blessing of the altar, it is to be noted that the exorcism of the water is done to drive out the enemy. For this blessing; four things are necessary, namely, water, wine, salt, and ashes; and this for three reasons.

8. First, because there are four things which chase the enemy. The first is the effusion of the tears that water represents. The second is the transport of the spiritual exultation that wine represents.

---

[348] John 15:5
[349] Tobit 13:22

The third, the natural discernment that salt represents. The fourth is the profound humility of ashes. So water is penance; wine, the exultation of the soul; salt, is wisdom, as has been established in the preceding chapter and the ashes, the humility of penance. This is why it is said of the Ninevites, that the king himself rose from his throne and put on a sackcloth and sat in ashes.[350] Then David said, 'I have eaten ashes like bread, etc.'[351] And Abraham said, 'I have taken upon me to speak unto the Lord, which am but dust and ashes.'[352]

9. Secondly, water is, in a way, the people or humanity, because the great waters are the multitude of peoples; wine is divinity; salt the doctrine of the divine law, which is the salt of the covenant; ashes, because they remind of the Lord's Passion. Wine mixed with water is Christ, God and man; and this takes place by the faith in the Lord's Passion, which we have by the doctrine of the divine law. The people, represented by water, are joined by the union of faith to their chief, God and man.

10. Thirdly, it may be said that this holy water signifies the Holy Spirit, without the breath and inspiration from which nothing is ever sanctified, and without the grace of which the remission of sins does not take place. Now, the very truth that the Holy Spirit is called water is shown when it says, 'He that believeth on me, as the scripture hath said, out of his belly shall flow rivers of living water.'[353] Which the Evangelist explains, when He says, 'Except a man be born of water and of the Spirit, etc.'[354]

11. The Church does not consecrate in the order of the sacrament externally by water alone, or internally by the Spirit alone; for, behold, the Lord says, 'Except a man be born of water and of the Spirit, etc.' This is the water, that is the Spirit. So in the sacrament of baptism, water is not without the Spirit, nor the Spirit without water, an element which the same Spirit sanctified, which in the first part of the creation of the world was on the waters.[355] Now, this water is sprinkled on the altar itself, and all around the outside

---

[350] See Jonah 3:6
[351] Psalm 102:9
[352] Genesis 18:27
[353] John 7:38
[354] John 3:5
[355] See Genesis 1:2

of the church when the church and the altar are dedicated at the same time.

12. Now although the Spirit and the water were sufficient for the perfection of baptism and the consecration of the church, yet the holy Fathers, who established this, wanted to satisfy us, not only with what relates to virtue but also to the sanctification of the sacrament. That is why they added salt, wine, oil, ashes and chrism. Philip, however, did not have the chrism and the oil when he baptized the eunuch.[356] Now, neither of these two things must be missed (the chrism and the oil), and we must mix them, because, without their union and their concurrence, the people of God (which is the Church) is neither sanctified nor delivered from sins. This will be touched on again in the chapter *Consecrations and Unctions*. With regards to the water, its necessity is, certainly, apparent, for it is said, 'Except a man be born, etc.'

13. Salt, because without the condiment of the faith that it represents, no one will ever be saved, regardless of how much one is sprinkled with the water of baptism. Wine refers to the spiritual intelligence of the divine law. This is why the Lord, at the wedding of Cana, changed the water into wine. If anyone is not sprinkled with this wine, that is to say, whoever does not drink of this wine or does not trust those who offer it to him, he will not reach the happiness of life eternal. Also the sprinkling of the ashes, by which one understands the humility of penance, is so necessary, that without it the remission of sins does not take place in adults; for by it they are prepared for baptism, and it is the only refuge open to sinners after baptism. This is why it is not without reason that the Lord, speaking of John in the Gospel, calls the name of baptism what He did, that He came into the whole region of Galilee preaching 'the baptism of repentance for the remission of sins.'[357] Notice that there are four kinds of holy water, which will be spoken of in Book Four, in the chapter *The Consecration and Aspersion of Holy Water*.

14. All these things being finished, the pontiff makes four crosses with the same water, on the four horns of the altar, and one in the middle. The four crosses represent the four kinds of charity

---

[356] See Acts 8:36-38
[357] Mark 1:4

that those who approach the altar must have, namely, to cherish God, themselves, their friends, and their enemies. Regarding these four horns of charity it is said, 'thou shalt spread abroad to the west, and to the east, and to the north, and to the south.'[358] And that is why we make four crosses at the four horns of the altar, to mark that Christ saved the four parts of the world by the Cross. Secondly, they are made to mark that we must carry the cross of the Lord in four ways, namely: in the heart, through meditation; in the mouth, by confession; in the body, by mortification; and on the forehead, by the assiduous impression of His sign. The cross made in the middle of the altar signifies the Passion that Christ endured in the middle of the earth, and through which He made salvation in the middle of the earth, that is, in Jerusalem.

15. Then the pontiff turns seven times around the altar. First, to show that he must take care of everything for all people, and have vigilance; this is designated by the circular movement. That is why we then sing, 'The watchmen that went about the city found me.'[359] He must, in fact, watch with solicitude the herds entrusted to him. For, as Gilbert says, 'it is a ridiculous thing to have a blind watchman, a lame runner, a negligent prelate, a doctor without science, and a mute public crier.'

16. Secondly, the seven circuits around the altar are the seven degrees of Christ's virtue of humility that we must have, and that we must run through frequently. The first virtue of Christ is that, from the rich, He has become poor; the second, that He was put in a manger; the third, that He was subjected to His parents; the fourth, that He bowed His head under the hand of a slave; the fifth, that He endured and suffered a disciple who was a thief and traitor; the sixth, how, full of gentleness, He appeared standing before an iniquitous judge; the seventh, that He prayed leniently for those who crucified Him.

17. Thirdly, the seven circuits around the altar represent the seven journeys of Christ. The first was from heaven into the womb of Mary. The second, from the womb of His mother to the manger. The third, from the cradle into the world. The fourth, from the

---

[358] Genesis 28:14
[359] Song of Songs 5:7

world to the gallows. The fifth, from the gibbet into the sepulchre. The sixth, from the sepulchre into the place of spirits. The seventh, from the place of spirits to heaven. Then the bishop sprinkles the altar.

18. Now the Apostle says what the altar in the temple means, 'for the temple of God is holy, which temple ye are.'[360] So if we are the temple of God, 'We have an altar.'[361] Our altar is our heart. For the heart is in a man what the altar is in the temple. On this altar is offered a sacrifice of praise and jubilation, according to this saying of the Psalmist, 'The sacrifices of God are a broken spirit, etc.'[362] On this altar is the commemoration of the Body and Blood of Christ. From this altar, prayers go up to heaven because God lowers His gaze upon our hearts. So, this altar is sprinkled with water, when the hearts of men are cleansed of their sins by the preaching of the gospel. For preaching is water, according to this saying, 'every one that thirsteth, come ye to the waters.'[363] So it is through this water, that is, through the preaching of the gospel and the sanctification of the Holy Spirit, that the altar of the heart and the whole man are both purified and made holy. Now, the altar of the heart is consecrated by the thought of fear, that it may be invited to good, and that by the effect of love it may be confirmed; for 'The fear of the Lord is the beginning of wisdom.'[364]

19. And the altar of water is sprinkled seven times, to show that in baptism the seven gifts of the Holy Spirit are granted to us. It also means that we must remember the Lord's Passion and always have it in our memory. For the seven sprinkles of water are the seven bestowals of the blood of Christ. The first took place during circumcision. The second while he was praying in the garden of olives and when His sweat changed into drops of blood. The third, when His body was flogged. The fourth, when His head was crowned with thorns. The fifth when His hands were pierced. The sixth, when His feet were nailed to the Cross. The seventh, when His side was opened. And there are some who

---

[360] 1 Corinthians 3:17
[361] Hebrews 13:10
[362] Psalm 51:17
[363] Isaiah 55:1
[364] Psalm 111:10

sprinkle three times because we baptise in the name of the Holy Trinity, or because the Church is purified of her sins by thought, word and deed; that is why we say the psalm 'Have mercy upon me, O God.'[365]

20. The sprinklings mentioned above are made with an aspersory made of hyssop, and this herb, which is lowly and grows in the earth, appropriately denotes the humility of Christ. Because the effusions of blood which we spoke of above were made with the hyssop of the humility of Christ and His inextinguishable charity, by which the Catholic Church, which has been sprinkled with it, is purified of its sins. This same herb grows naturally in stone, and the humility of nature grew in Christ, the Living Stone. For, according to the Apostle, 'that rock was Christ.'[366] Hyssop is also of a warm nature, and the humility of Christ has set cold hearts on fire with the exercise of the works of charity. Its roots penetrate the rocks, and humility breaks down the obstacles that stop the man who does not practice charity. It is good for the chest and against swelling, and Jesus Christ heals the swelling of pride. It is born and takes root in the earth; that is why we can understand by it all the multitude of the faithful; and certainly, they are well represented by hyssop, those who, rooted and founded in the faith of Christ, cannot be uprooted and separated from His love. Also by these men, who can we better understand than the bishops and priests, who, the higher they are raised in dignity in the Church, the more strongly they must attach themselves to the faith of Christ? Certainly, it is through them that the water is sprinkled, it is through them also, and by their hands, that the faithful of Christ are baptized. It is to them, finally, that it has been given to perfect the ceremonies (*sacramenta*) of baptism.

21. While the altar is sprinkled with water, the bishop sings, 'This house is a house of prayer, etc.,'[367] and again, 'I will declare thy name unto my brethren.'[368] And because no work can come to its consummation without God, he prays, that those who come to this place to ask for graces may have them granted. Therefore,

---

[365] Psalm 51
[366] 1 Corinthians 10:4
[367] See Matthew 21:13
[368] Psalm 22:22

when the church and the altar are consecrated together, the whole church is sprinkled with water, as it was said in the previous chapter. Then, having done so, the pontiff approaches the altar with the Psalmist, and pours the rest of the water at the foot of the altar; as in the Old Testament, the remaining blood was poured into the channel, which is the same as the base or the foot of the altar.[369] Which means that we put back into the hands of God what remains and what surpasses human power in such a great sacrament and that it is entrusted to Him who is the Supreme Priest, and whose part it is to make up for the defects of other priests. The sepulchre, or the hole in which the relics must be enclosed, represents the golden urn full of manna that had been placed in the Ark of the Testimony, as it was said in the chapter, *The Altar and its Parts*. Now this kind of sepulchre, which some call a confession, is our heart, and we consecrate it with four crosses made of chrism.

22. Because there are four virtues described in the book of Wisdom; these are prudence, strength, temperance, and justice, which are, in a sense, four unctions which our heart receives when, by the gift of the Holy Spirit, it is prepared to receive the mysteries of the secrets of heaven. The sepulchre is sometimes made at the upper part of the altar, and sometimes at the anterior side.

23. Surely, the consecration of a fixed altar, but also of a travelling or portable altar, does not take place without the relics of the saints, or, when one cannot have them in a particular place, without the body of Christ.[370] For the martyrs and the lives of the confessors passionately followed the examples of the two Testaments, and their relics have been left to us to remind us to imitate them. We enclose them in a coffer or a chest when we hold them in our hearts to imitate them. So that if we hear and understand them, and do not put what they teach into practice, it is more for our condemnation than for our salvation, 'For not the hearers of the law are just before God, but the doers of the law

---

[369] See Exodus 29:12
[370] See chapter 2

THE DEDICATION OF THE ALTAR

shall be justified.'[371] This is why the Apostle says, 'Be ye followers of me, even as I also am of Christ.'[372]

24. Now the solemn bearing of the relics takes place in imitation of what is read in Exodus.[373] On the Ark of the Testament, there were two rings of gold which penetrated all the wood, and golden sticks of sethin were brought in, and they were used to carry the Ark. Now before the pontiff enters his church, he goes around it with the relics, so that they may be the protectors of this church. It is also read in the book of Kings that, at the dedication of the temple, all the elders of Israel were gathered together. Also the princes or chiefs of the tribes, and the dukes of the families, and they came to King Solomon at Jerusalem to witness the translation of the Ark of the Covenant of the Lord, and all the elders of Israel also came. The priests carried the ark of the Lord's covenant into His house and into the oracle of the temple, in the Holy of Holies, under the wings of the cherubim. For the cherubim spread their wings over the place occupied by the ark and covered the ark and the sticks that held it. Then King Solomon, and all the multitude of the people of Israel that were gathered with him came with him before the ark. In memory of which, the prelates, the great and the judges of the today go to the dedication of the churches, and follow the bishop consecrator in the procession, and the priests solemnly carry the relics under a flag or umbrella. Then the pontiff, before entering with his suite into the church, makes a sermon to the people. For Solomon, after the ark was brought to the temple, turned to the people and blessed all the congregation of Israel, and prayed for those who pray in the church. And all the people of Israel stood, and Solomon said, 'Blessed be the Lord, God of Israel, etc.,' as it is read in the same place.[374]

25. We store the relics of the saints with three grains of incense in a box because we must recall the examples of the saints with faith in the Trinity, that is, of the Father, the Son, and the Holy Spirit. For we must believe one God, one faith, and one baptism;

---

[371] Romans 2:13

[372] 1 Corinthians 11:1 The KJV translated as 'followers' comes from the Greek *mimetes*, 'to imitate.'

[373] Exodus 25:12 Refers to four rings not two

[374] 1 Kings 8:2-6, 8, 15

because 'The just shall live by faith,'[375] without which, as the Apostle has said, 'it is impossible to please him.'[376] Placed upon and fitted to this sepulchre is a tablet with the sign of the cross marked on it with chrism. For by the chrism we understand the gift of the Holy Spirit by which the tablet, that is charity, is anointed on its surface, because our heart is established by the grace of the Holy Spirit, so that it can observe the mysteries of heaven. Therefore the tablet, provided with this sign, is placed on the relics, because, by the examples of the saints, charity ignites; this charity which 'shall cover the multitude of sins,'[377] just as the tablet covers the relics. Which made the Apostle say, 'the love of God is shed abroad in our hearts by the Holy Ghost which is given unto us.'[378] This tablet or stone contains or is called the seal of the sepulchre, as Pope Alexander III says. Then we put on the altar the stone called the table of the altar. Through it, we can understand the perfection and solidity of the knowledge of God. This must be of stone, not because of the hardness but of the solidity of faith, according to what the Lord said to Peter, 'thou art Peter, and upon this rock,' that is to say, on this unshakable firmness of faith, 'I will build my church.'[379]

26. Thus, just as the table is the confirmation and perfection of the altar, so the knowledge of God is the confirmation and perfection of all good works. This is why it is said to God in Wisdom, 'For to know thee is perfect justice: and to know thy justice, and thy power, is the root of immortality.'[380] Also the Lord says, through the mouth of Jeremiah, 'But let him that glorieth glory in this, that he understandeth and knoweth me.'[381]

27. By the same stone, one understands Christ, whose Apostle says, 'Jesus Christ himself being the chief corner stone,'[382] Now, the stone designates the humanity of Christ, and one reads of Him in Daniel that 'Thou sawest till that a stone was cut out

---

[375] Romans 1:17
[376] Hebrews 11:6
[377] 1 Peter 4:8
[378] Romans 5:5
[379] Matthew 16:18
[380] Wisdom 15:3
[381] Jeremiah 9:24
[382] Ephesians 2:20

without hands.'³⁸³ Because Christ was born in an admirable way, (*sine virili semine*) of the Blessed Virgin (who, because of the eminence of her virtues, is called a mountain), and become a great mountain. He has filled the whole orb of the earth. The Psalmist also says, regarding Him, 'The stone which the builders refused is become the head stone of the corner.'³⁸⁴ Because Christ, whom the architects, that is to say, the Jews, had rejected, saying, 'We will not have this man to reign over us.'³⁸⁵ became the head of the corner because, as the Apostle says, 'Wherefore God also hath highly exalted him, etc.'³⁸⁶ Or else, by the stone one understands charity, as has been said above. Charity, indeed, is the stone which must be large and broad, for the precept of charity is extended, since it extends to particular enemies, according to this precept of the Lord, 'Love your enemies.'³⁸⁷

28. Only stone altars are anointed because the altar represents Christ, who is a Stone growing into a mountain, as has been said. Of Him it is written, 'thy God, hath anointed thee with the oil of gladness above thy fellows.'³⁸⁸ However, one reads in Exodus that the Lord commanded to make wooden altars of shittim,³⁸⁹ which cannot decay;³⁹⁰ that is why the side altars of the church are of wood. Solomon also made a golden altar, as it is read in the book of Kings,³⁹¹ but these altars were figures. And, in the county of Provence, in the village of Sainte-Marie-de-la-Mer, there is an altar of earth that Mary Magdalene and Martha, and Mary the mother of James and Mary Salome made there. After that, and when one has sprinkled the altar and baptised it with water, it remains to anoint it with oil and chrism. Now the bishop pours on the oil and the chrism, and he sings, 'Jacob rose up early in the morning, and took the stone that he had put for his pillows, and set it up for a pillar, and poured oil upon the top of it,'³⁹² for this

---

[383] Daniel 2:34
[384] Psalm 118:22
[385] Luke 19:14
[386] Philippians 2:9
[387] Matthew 5:44
[388] Psalm 45:7
[389] Acacia
[390] Exodus 27:1
[391] See 1 Kings 6:22
[392] Genesis 28:18

church was the type of others, 'for out of Zion shall go forth the law, and the word of the Lord from Jerusalem.'[393]

29. The bishop first makes five crosses on the altar with the oil of the infirm, according to the Roman order. However, according to certain other churches, he makes one cross of oil in the middle of the altar, and four in the four corners. Then he does the same thing and as many times with the chrism. Assuredly, by oil one must understand the grace of the Holy Spirit. The prophet Isaiah said, speaking of this oil, 'the yoke shall be destroyed because of the anointing,'[394] because, just as the bishop pours the oil on the altar, so does Christ, who is the Chief High Priest, pour grace on our altar, which is our heart. For He distributes all graces by the Holy Spirit, as the Apostle says, 'For to one is given by the Spirit the word of wisdom; to another the word of knowledge, etc.'[395] Also as the bishop purifies the table of the altar with the oil, so the Holy Spirit purifies our heart of all from all vices and sins.

30. Christ was also anointed with oil, not visible in truth, but invisible, that is, with the grace of the Holy Spirit. Which made David say, 'thy God, hath anointed thee with the oil of gladness above thy fellows.'[396] that is to say, more than all the saints who have been partakers of His Grace, that is Christ. That is why the anointing is more specifically suited to Christ than to others; because, above all others. God anointed Him so that He had the fullness of good things, and that is why it is said that He was the Anointed One. The anointing done with the oil also means mercy, according to this word of the Gospel, 'anoint thine head, and wash thy face.'[397] For, like oil in liquids, so mercy in good works always rises above (is superior to) good works; and whatever liquid you pour on oil, it always floats on the surface. Also, regarding mercy, it is written, 'The Lord is good to all: and his tender mercies are over all his works,'[398] and 'mercy rejoiceth against judgment.'[399] Let the altar of our heart be anointed with

---

[393] Isaiah 2:3
[394] Isaiah 10:27
[395] 1 Corinthians 12:8
[396] Psalm 45:7
[397] Matthew 6:17
[398] Psalm 145:9
[399] James 2:13

this oil, so that, always keeping the remembrance of mercy, we should not lose the grace of the sprinkling of water, of regeneration, and of baptism.

31. The five crosses of oil signify that we must always have present the memory of the five wounds of Christ, which He suffered for us on the Cross. For He received five wounds, namely, on His hands, feet, and side. They also designate the five kinds of suffering of mercy that we need.

32. For it is necessary for man to have pity on Christ by sympathizing with His Passion, which made Job say in the person of Christ, 'Have pity upon me, have pity upon me, O ye my friends; etc.'[400] It is also necessary that man should have pity on his neighbour, whose evils he sees, on which we read in Ecclesiasticus, 'The compassion of man is toward his neighbour.'[401] And this in three ways, namely: for the sins of commission, while lamenting them, which made Jeremiah say, 'no man repented him of his wickedness, saying, What have I done?'[402] For the omissions, on which Isaiah said, 'Woe is me! for I am undone; because I am a man of unclean lips;'[403] as if he said, 'Because I have omitted the good that I have been able to do,' and good works done in a spirit in a less pure manner than they should have been. This is why St Luke says, 'when ye shall have done all those things which are commanded you, say, We are unprofitable servants,' etc.'[404] As if he said, 'We have done good works, but not well, not purely, and that is why we have done them uselessly; like one who, giving alms for glory alone, does good, but not good, not purely so. Ecclesiasticus, speaking of this triple pity, says, 'Have pity on thy own soul, pleasing God.'[405] Now one makes two crosses to mark that true pity of the soul must accompany the accomplishment of good work. The first cross is made with oil, and the second with chrism; which comes from where the psalm says, 'A good man sheweth favour, and

---

[400] Job 19:21
[401] Ecclesiasticus 18:12
[402] Jeremiah 8:6
[403] Isaiah 6:5 The Vulgate has, 'Woe is me, because I have held my peace.'
[404] Luke 17:10
[405] Ecclesiasticus. 30:24

lendeth: he will guide his affairs with discretion.'[406] In addition, as it is not sufficient to have compassion in the soul together with the practice of the good work without the aroma of good repute, according to this word of the Gospel, 'Let your light so shine before men, that they may see your good works, and glorify your Father which is in heaven.'[407] That is why we make crosses with the chrism, which consists of balm and oil.

33. Now, the balm, because of its good aroma, signifies good repute; oil, because of its clarity, the brightness of the consciousness that we must have, according to this word of the Apostle, 'our rejoicing is this, the testimony of our conscience.'[408] The balm is well united with the oil when the good aroma (of repute) is united with mercy.

34. We also understand, through the five crosses of oil and chrism, the five senses of our body, which are doubled and rise to the value of ten. Because, sometimes, by making good use of the senses of our body, we keep both ourselves, and by our example and our teaching, we confirm others, in the practice of good works. That is why the good steward would boast, saying, 'behold, I have gained beside them five talents more.'[409] and while we make these anointings of which we have spoken above, we sing, 'God, even thy God, hath anointed thee, etc.;'[410] which is said of Christ. So the altar is anointed three times, twice with oil, and the third time with chrism, because the church is illustrated by faith, hope and charity, which are greater than other virtues. While the chrism is poured out, they sing, 'the smell of my son is as the smell of a field.'[411] This field is the Church, which is engrossed with flowers, shines with virtues, and is embalmed by the perfume of its good works. There are the roses of the martyrs, the lilies of the virgins, the violets of the confessors, and the turf of those who are beginning. After the anointing, they burn incense, which signifies the devotion of prayer, and he who has

---

[406] Psalm 112:5
[407] Matthew 5:16
[408] 2 Corinthians 1:12
[409] Matthew 25:20
[410] Hebrews 1:9
[411] Genesis 27:27

the seven gifts of the Holy Spirit has made himself like God, so he can offer a devout prayer to Him whose image he is.[412]

35. Incense is burned in five places, namely, at the four corners and in the middle of the altar, because we must exercise the five senses of the body so that the repute of our good work extends to our neighbour. Regarding this, the Apostle says, 'For we are unto God a sweet savour of Christ, in them that are saved, and in them that perish.'[413] And in the Gospel, 'Let your light shine, etc.' This frequent use of incense is also the continual prayer that Christ, Priest and Pontiff, addresses for us to God the Father.

36. To make the cross with incense is to exhibit His suffering to the Father and Him interceding for us. The copious burning of incense in the middle and at the corners of the altar is to multiply the prayers in Jerusalem and the universal Church.

37. Then the bishop confirms the altar with the sign of the cross, saying, 'Confirm this altar, O Lord, etc.' This confirmation made with the chrism by the pontiff, on the front surface of the stone, signifies the confirmation which is performed every day by the Holy Spirit, through charity, on the altar of the heart, so that no tribulation can separate our soul from the love of God. This is why the Apostle says, 'Who shall separate us from the love of Christ? shall tribulation, or distress, etc.'[414] Then the *Gloria Patri* is sung in praise to the Trinity.

38. The final blessing of the altar represents the final blessing that will take place when it is said, 'Come, ye blessed of my Father, etc.'[415] Then, the altar is wiped with a white linen cloth, to mark that we must purify our hearts by a chaste life. Then we bless the vessels, the sacred vestments and the linen consecrated to the divine worship; for Moses was instructed by the Lord for forty days on how to make the necessary cloths and ornaments for the temple.[416]

---

[412] This refers to one who has received not just the outer and physical sign but the inner and spiritual grace

[413] 2 Corinthians 2:14

[414] Romans 8:35

[415] Matthew 25:34

[416] Here is a good example of how an apparent incongruity, illogical or seemingly nonsensical statement in spiritual writing often points to there being a deeper mystical understanding. In this instance why would it take forty days for God to teach Moses about how to make the cloths and

39. Now to bless the utensils of the church is to bring our works to God. After that, the altar is dressed with clean white cloths. This has been spoken of in the chapter, *The Altar*. Finally, we adorn the church and light the lamps and candle, because then the works of the righteous will shine. 'The just shall shine, and shall run to and fro like sparks among the reeds.'[417] Then, with the altar having been consecrated in this way, we celebrate Mass and offer sacrifice. to the Most High. It is this sacrifice of which the prophet says, 'The sacrifices of God are a broken spirit: a broken and a contrite heart, etc.;[418] as I will say in the *Preface* to Book Four. However, consecration should not take place without Mass, according to Pope Gelasius, because then the sacrament is revealed, which was hidden even from the angels from the beginning. Again, notice that during the aspersion of the church the pontiff only uses linen and the most common clothes. For the Mass, however, he is adorned with pontifical and precious vestments, reminding you that the high priest of the law purified the sanctuary in a linen ephod and that after having washed and dressed himself in the high priest's robes, he made the burnt offering of rams. But as, after the purification, he was clothed in the same linen ephod to send away the scapegoat,[419] that is why even today, for the consecration of the fonts and immersion of the catechumens, where their sins are transferred, there are some who use common clothes and linen vestments.

---

ornaments for the temple? Forty is a number of mystical significance. In addition, the reader is being directed towards seeking a detailed understanding of the symbolism of these cloths and ornaments

[417] Wisdom 3:7
[418] Psalm 51:17
[419] See Leviticus 16

8 CONSECRATIONS AND UNCTIONS

1. It is read that the Lord commanded Moses to compose an oil, 'chrism,' (*chrisma*) to anoint the tabernacle on the day of the dedication, as well as the Ark of the Testament, the table and the sacred vessels; finally, to consecrate, by a similar anointing, the priests and kings.[420]

2. One does not read, however, that Moses was anointed with other than a spiritual anointing, as was Christ. Now Christ did not wish to be anointed with the material unction since it is through Him that we receive the spiritual unction with which He was anointed. That is why the Church, merciful mother, makes various anointings. We shall touch on this here in passing, and say, first, what these anointings signify and second, what they consist of. Thirdly, we will speak of the anointing we do to those we are to baptise. Fourth, of the anointing which is done to those who are baptized, an unction with which the bishop marks them on the forehead. Fifth the unction of those being ordained priests. Sixth, of the anointing which serves to consecrate the bishops and the princes. Seventh, of that of the church, of the altar, of the chalice, and of the other vessels devoted to the divine worship. Eighth, of extreme unction; ninth, for the consecration and blessing of the cemetery, vestments and other ornaments of the church. Tenth, of the consecration and blessing of the virgins.

3. First, it should be noted that there are two kinds of anointing: the external, which is material or corporeal and visible, and the internal, which is spiritual and invisible. The body is visibly anointed by the external unction. The Apostle St James says about

---

[420] See Exodus 30:22-37

the first, 'Is any sick among you? let him call for the elders of the church; and let them pray over him, anointing him with oil in the name of the Lord: And the prayer of faith shall save the sick.'[421] The Apostle St John says of the second, 'But the anointing which ye have received of him abideth in you, and ye need not that any man teach you: but as the same anointing teacheth you of all things, and is truth, and is no lie, etc.'[422] The interior unction is not only a sign, that is to say the signification of a thing, but it is also a sacrament, because if it is worthily received, it gives, or it increases, without any doubt, what it represents, that is, the salvation of body and soul according to this saying, 'they shall lay hands on the sick, and they shall recover.'[423] In the second place, it is necessary to know that one blesses two oils to make the external and visible unction. These are the holy oil or the oil of the catechumens, with which catechumens are anointed, and the oil of the sick, which one anoints the sick with. The authority of St James, above, says this, 'Is any of you sick? etc.' It will be said in Book Six, in the chapter *The Same Thursday of the Lord's Supper*, how the blessings of both oils and chrism are made.

4. But one may ask why we anoint the infirm and the catechumens with oil? I answer that it is so that, by visible things, the invisible ones can be seized more easily. For just as oil, by driving away sickness, gives new life to tired members, and its nature serves to illuminate by the light it produces; so it is necessary to believe that the anointing of the consecrated oil, which is the sign of faith, by putting away sins, gives health to the soul and enlightens it. So the visible oil, in the outward sign, is the invisible oil in the inward sacrament, and the spiritual oil within the body. Regarding the oil of the sick, we received authority from the Apostles. As for the oil of the catechumens, we have men who have succeeded the Apostles.[424]

5. Although God may grant the spiritual oil without one receiving the physical, however, as the Apostles for the sick, and their successors for the catechumens, have made use of this means, we

---

[421] James 5:14-15
[422] 1 John 2:27
[423] Mark 16:18
[424] Referring to those who have experienced the spiritual enlightenment of the Apostles

cannot omit this without sinning against what their authority has consecrated, as has been said in the chapter *The Altar and its Parts*. For it was in this way that the righteous once pleaded with God, first without being circumcised; but when God had made a command of circumcision, those who omitted it were committing a sin. Thirdly, let us speak of the function of those to be baptized. Now, in the New Testament, not only kings and priests are anointed, as will soon be said, but also all Christians, because Christ made us kings and priests in His blood before our God. That is to say, priest-kings, according to what St Peter says, 'But ye are a chosen generation,' that is, chosen from men; 'a royal priesthood,'[425] which you possess in conducting yourself well.

6. All Christians are anointed twice with holy oil before their baptism. First on the chest, then between the shoulders, and twice after baptism, with consecrated chrism. First by the priest, on the top of the head and then by the bishop, on the forehead. According to St Augustine, the first three anointings which the Church does have been introduced more by usage than by virtue of some testimony of scripture. Now, we anoint the one to be baptized on the chest, the seat of the heart; first, so that, by the gift of the Holy Spirit, he rejects error and ignorance and receives the right faith, because 'The just shall live by faith,'[426] and 'with the heart man believeth unto righteousness.'[427] Then between the shoulders, so that, by the grace of the Holy Spirit, he shakes off laziness and negligence, and exercises the practice of good works. Because 'faith without works is dead;'[428] so that, by the mystery (*sacramentum*) of faith, his thoughts become increasingly purified. Again, on the chest, so that by exercising good works, he has the strength to support the labours of this life. On the shoulders, since faith 'worketh by love,'[429] according to the Apostle. Now the oil thus passes from the heart to the shoulders, and the faith which is conceived in one's soul arrives at its perfection by works; because, according to this definition, faith is doing what you say. Also he who has been baptized is anointed by the priest on the

---

[425] 1 Peter 2:9
[426] Romans 1:17
[427] Romans 10:10
[428] James 2:26
[429] Galatians 5:6

top of his head, in order to be ready to give the reason for his faith to every man who questions him.[430] By head, we understand the soul, according to what we read, 'The eyes,' that is to say, the intelligence, 'of the wise man are in his head,'[431] that is, in his soul, whose upper part is reason, and the lower is sensuality. That is why, by the top of the head, which is its upper part, we rightly understand reason, which is the highest part of the soul. We will speak of this later, in Book Six, in the chapter *Holy Saturday*, where we deal with Confirmation. Now, before baptism, the man is anointed with holy oil, and after with holy chrism, for the chrism is suitable only for the Christian.

7. Christ (*Christus*) takes His name from the chrism or from the unction (*chrismate*) He received; or rather it is from Christ (*Christo*) that this anointing took its name (*chrisma*) from, not according to the form of the name only, but rather according to the rule of law. Christians derive their name from Christ, as in the same way the anointings derive from the anointed (*uncti ab uncto*), that is to say from Christ. Thus all gather to the smell of the unguent of Christ, whose name is as widespread oil; but according to the power of the word, Christians are called so from 'chrism,' according to Isidore. This will be discussed in the *Preface* to Book Two.

8. According to St Augustine, the first anointing made with oil also shows that we are prepared to understand the whole faith, and that we are called to the good odour of Christ and warned to renounce the devil. The second anointing is done on the chest and between the shoulders, according to Rabanus,[432] so that by faith we are fortified on all sides and filled with courage, to complete good works with the grace of God. For by the chest is meant the virtue of faith. By the shoulders, on which burdens are borne, is understood in a clear manner the strength of man and the practice of good works, according to this saying, 'they bind heavy burdens and grievous to be borne, and lay them on men's

---

[430] See 1 Peter 3:15
[431] Ecclesiastes 2:14
[432] Rabanus Maurus Magnentius (c. 780 – 856), a Benedictine monk and theologian who became archbishop of Mainz, Germany. Composer of the *Veni Creator Spiritus* (Come Creator Spirit). One English translation of this is the hymn 'Come, Holy Ghost, our souls inspire.'

CONSECRATIONS AND UNCTIONS

shoulders, etc.'[433] So a man is anointed on the chest and between the shoulders, so that he leaves the works of the devil behind him in spirit and in practice, and so that he is able to understand the word of God and robustly to carry his yoke and the burden of the law.

9. The anointing that is done on the summit of the head, that is, the top of the head, over the brain, takes place, according to the same author, so that the one who is anointed is worthy to participate in the heavenly kingdom, and because the soul of the baptized man is betrothed to his head who is Christ. It is because of this that we anoint with the chrism, which is itself composed of oil and balm, so that we know that the Spirit, which operates in an invisible way, is given to this man. Now oil warms the tired limbs and gives light, as was said above, and balm exhales a good odour. Assuredly, souls are tired when they repent from turning against God; the Holy Spirit then comes to them. He illuminates their intelligence and clearly shows them that their sins have been or must be given to Him. At the same time He gives them the gift of good works which breathe into others a good odour; which is the perfumed balm. It is also because the seat of pride always opens up to the highest views, according to the meaning of its very name,[434] which seems to be on the top of the head, that rightly this part of the body is anointed with the shape of a cross and represents humility.

10. Pope Sylvester decided that this unction would be administered by priests to one on the verge of death. From this one can believe that before this time two anointings, on the summit of the head and the forehead, were reserved for the bishop. Because, as the bosom of the Church was extended and it was no longer possible for the bishops to confirm everyone, this pope established, so that the faithful might not die without being anointed with the chrism, that they should be anointed by priests on the crown of the head. That is, over the brain, which is the seat of wisdom, and that for the strengthening and increase of grace, 'so that, if they die afterwards,' says Sicard of

---

[433] Matthew 23:4
[434] Referring to the Latin: *superbia ... superiora aperit* which translates as *pride ... opens higher*

Cremona,[435] 'they receive in proportion to grace the increase of glory.'

11. Nevertheless we believe that, without receiving the unction, one is saved by baptism alone, and that, although he is not concerned with the laying on of hands, God gives the Holy Spirit to whom He wishes to give it, as it says in the Acts of the Apostles.

12. The followers of Arnaud (of Bresse or Brescia[436]), heretics full of deceit, maintain that men never receive the Holy Spirit through baptism with water, and that the baptized Samaritans only received it when one had laid hands on them. Now, according to Rabanus, two anointings are made in the form of a cross, so that from that moment the devil, recognizing on the vessel that had first belonged to him, the sign of his first defeat, (that of the holy cross), by which he been conquered, may know that he is from then of Another (*alienum*). That is to say that he has become alienated (*alienatum*) from him.

13. It is also said, according to him, that the anointing on the chest invokes the Trinity, so that no trace of the enemy remains hidden in the heart of man. But that, by faith in the Holy Trinity, his soul is strengthened, and both receives and understands the commandments of God. So every believer is anointed twice, first of all with oil; then, in the same way, twice with the chrism. First, in baptism, at the top of the head; secondly, after baptism, on the forehead, at Confirmation, because the Spirit was given twice to the Apostles, as will be said in Book Six, in the chapter *Holy Saturday*. Fourth, we should speak of the anointing that the bishop does on the forehead but this will be dealt with in Book Six, in the chapter *Holy Saturday*.

14. Fifth, with regard to the anointing of those to be ordained, it should be noted that the hands of the priest are anointed by the bishop, so that he may know that in this sacrament he receives from the Holy Spirit the virtue and grace to consecrate. That is why the bishop, anointing his hands, says to him, 'Lord, deign to

---

[435] Gerard of Cremona (c. 1114–1187) was an Italian translator of scientific books from Arabic into Latin

[436] Arnaud de Bresse, a native of the city of Bresse, Italy, and a heretic, lived in the twelfth century. His adherents were given the names of Poplicians, Publicans, and Arnaldists

consecrate and sanctify these hands by this anointing and by our blessing, so that all they consecrate will be consecrated, and all that they blessed be blessed in the name of the Lord.' That is why devout people kiss the hands of the priests immediately after their ordination, because they believe that, in doing so, they participate in their prayers and good works. Now the hands of the priests are anointed with consecrated oil, because they must, according to their strength, exercise all the works of mercy. For the hands designate works, the oil mercy. This is why the Samaritan, in dressing the wounded, poured wine and oil on his wounds.[437] Also, the hands are anointed again with oil, so that they may be clean to offer to God the host for sins, and to fill widely, and not in a dry and low way, the other Offices of piety and mercy. Oil also represents the grace of healing and the charity of diligence. That is why we also impose the hands with the oil on the head of the one who is ordained, because by the fingers we understand the gifts of the Holy Spirit, and by the head the soul of the recipient. The hands are therefore imposed on the priest, because he who is penetrated with the gifts of the Holy Spirit is destined to do the works of Christ.

15. Sixth, with regard to the anointing of bishops and princes, it must be known that the function of bishops has its origin in the Old Testament. For it is said, 'the high priest among his brethren, upon whose head the anointing oil was poured, etc."[438] Surely we anoint the bishop with the chrism, which, as we have said above, is made of oil and balm, and he is anointed both on the body and in the heart. Thus he has inside the brightness of conscience before God, and externally the odour of good repute in front of his neighbour. The first is designated by oil, the second by the balm. Touching on the brightness of consciousness, the Apostle says, 'For our rejoicing is this, the testimony of our conscience.'[439]

---

[437] See Luke 10:34
[438] Leviticus 21:10 The Vulgate has, 'The high priest, that is to say, the priest who is the greatest among his brethren, upon whose head the oil of unction hath been poured; and whose hands have been consecrated for the priesthood.'
[439] 2 Corinthians 1:12

Also, 'The king's daughter is all glorious within,'[440] that is, proceeds from his soul. The same Apostle says, speaking of the odour of good repute, 'For we are unto God a sweet savour of Christ; in them that are saved, and in them that perish:'[441] that is to say, that we imitate His example in every place, and that, 'To the one we are the savour of death unto death; and to the other the savour of life unto life.'[442] As if he said, 'We are an example of the diligence and the good thought that leads to eternal life; for others, we are an odour of death that leads to death, that is, an exhalation of envy and bad thought that leads to eternal death.'

16. Now the bishop must have a 'good testimony' in him, to both people who are in the church and 'those who are outside.'[443] For just as one curtain draws another after it,[444] so the faithful must draw after them the unfaithful to faith, and he who listens to it, learning and believing, should say to him, 'Come,'[445] by advocating the faith. Also one consecrates the head and the hands of the bishop with this perfume (the chrism); for by the head you understand the soul, according to this word of the Gospel, 'Anoint thine head,' that is to say, humble your head, 'and wash your face'[446] with your tears. These works, according to these words, are read in the Canticles, 'My hands,' which are my good works, have 'dropped with myrrh,'[447] that is to say, have given others a good example.

17. The head is anointed with the balm of charity. First, so that the bishop may cherish God with all his heart, and with all his mind, and with all his soul; and also, following the example of Christ, his neighbour as himself, that is to say, as much as himself. Oil on the head is charity in the soul, according to St Gregory. Secondly, the anointing of the head marks authority and dignity, because one consecrates not only a bishop, but also a king. Thirdly, in order to show by this that he represents (as His vicar)

---

[440] Psalm 45:13 The Vulgate has, 'All the glory of the king's daughter is within.' (Ps. 44:14)
[441] 2 Corinthians 2:15
[442] 2 Corinthians 2:16
[443] 1 Timothy 3:7
[444] See Exodus 26:3
[445] Revelation 22:17
[446] Matthew 6:17
[447] Song of Songs 5:5

the person of Christ, the one of whom it is said by the prophet, 'the precious ointment upon the head, etc.'[448] Now the head of man is Christ; the head of Christ is God, of whom He Himself says, 'The Spirit of the Lord is upon me, because he hath anointed me to preach the gospel to the poor.'[449] So Christ, our head, is anointed with the invisible oil; He appeals to the universal Church on every occasion and for all, and the bishop has this power only for what has been entrusted to him.

18. The hands are anointed to confer the ministry and the charge of the episcopate. For they anoint the hands with oil which designate the works, and this oil is the chrism of piety and mercy. First, so that the bishop will do good to everyone, but especially to those who are of the household of faith,[450] that they may not be closed to anyone, but that they be open to all, according to this saying, 'She stretcheth out her hand to the poor; yea, she reacheth forth her hands to the needy.'[451] The arid hand, the miserly hand, the hand paralyzed by shrivelling cannot open. The hands are anointed, that they may be healed, that they may open, and that they may pour out alms into the bosom of the needy. Secondly, to show that the bishop receives the power to bless and consecrate. Therefore, when he who consecrates him anoints his hands, he says, 'Lord, deign to consecrate and sanctify these hands, etc.,' as above. Third, that they may be pure to offer the hosts for sins. Notice that although the bishop's hands were oil-rich when ordained priest, yet they are anointed again with the chrism when consecrated bishop. In fact, the hands are the works, the oil is the abundance of the Holy Spirit and of grace, by the balm that is joined to it and mixed with it; the smell of good repute is represented by chrism. We read in Ecclesiasticus, 'my odour is as the purest balm.'[452] Now, just as, in the heavenly hierarchy, the higher angels by rank possess a greater grace than

---

[448] Psalm 133:2
[449] Luke 4:18
[450] See Galatians 6:10
[451] Proverbs 31:20 Prov. 31:10-11 indicates that the 'she' in the following verses relates to a virtuous woman or wife. Both priests and nuns are 'brides of Christ' so the feminine here is not out of context, particularly in light of the preceding paragraph
[452] Ecclesiasticus 24:21

the good angels who are inferior to them, so, in the works of bishops and other men raised in dignity, the gift of the Holy Spirit must appear more than in their inferiors. Also the perfume of good repute must be exhaled more sweetly, according to this word of the Second Letter to the Corinthians, 'we are unto God a sweet savour of Christ.'[453] That is why, when the bishops are consecrated, their hands, anointed with oil, are anointed with chrism, and with good reason.

19. The thumb is anointed with the chrism, so that by its imposition it benefits everyone for salvation.

20. Now, in the Old Testament, we anointed not only the priest, but also the king and the prophet, as we see in the book of Kings. Therefore the Lord gave this commandment to Elijah, 'Go, return on thy way to the wilderness of Damascus: and when thou comest, anoint Hazael to be king over Syria: And Jehu the son of Nimshi shalt thou anoint to be king over Israel: and Elisha the son of Shaphat of Abelmeholah shalt thou anoint to be prophet in thy room.'[454] Samuel also anointed David to make him king. But after Jesus the Nazarene, whom God anointed with the Holy Spirit, as it is read in the Acts of the Apostles, was anointed with oil over His companions,[455] who, according to the Apostle, is the head of the Church which is the body of this same prince,[456] the anointing now passed from head to arm. So since Christ the prince has not been anointed on the head, but on the arm or shoulder, or at the joint of the arm and the shoulder, which rightly represents the commandment. For we read, 'the government shall be upon his shoulder, etc.'[457] It was to mark this, that Samuel placed a shoulder in front of Saul, whom he had placed at the end of the table,[458] in the presence of all the guests. Now, we observe anointing the head of the pontiff with oil, because he represents

---

[453] 2 Corinthians 2:15
[454] 1 Kings 19:15-16
[455] See Acts 4:27, Hebrews 1:9
[456] See Ephesians 5:23
[457] Isaiah 9:6
[458] See 1 Samuel 9:22-24

in his charge the person of the Head (*capitis*), that is, the Christ, who is the head (*caput*) of the Church.[459]

21. There is, however, this difference between the anointing of the pontiff and the prince, in that the head of the pontiff is consecrated with chrism, but that the prince's arm is rubbed with oil. This is to show how much the power of the prince differs from the authority of the pontiff. Also observe that, just as one reads in the gospels that a father of the family called his servants, and gave them ten pieces of silver; so the vocation of the servant is the canonical election of the bishop, which is according to the word of the Lord, when He called Aaron. A piece of silver is given to him, when the one who took charge of these sums gives him the book of the Gospel, saying, 'Go, preach.' And when he enters for the first time in his metropolitan city, he carries the Gospel on his breast, according to the custom of certain churches, presenting and showing, like the intendant, the sum of money entrusted to him. In some churches too, when the archbishop gives him the staff, he says to him, 'Go, preach,' and immediately he blesses the people; which signifies how Moses was sent with the rod to Egypt.

22. The bishops are also accustomed, on the day of their consecration, to mount horses covered with white covers; which represents what we read in the Apocalypse, 'the armies which were in heaven followed him upon white horses.'[460] Certainly, the troops who are in heaven, are the good ones and righteous men, and prelates, who every day follow, according to the heavenly views, God in all the good works they do. It is said for that reason that they are in heaven, because they cherish and seek only heavenly goods, which made the Apostle say, 'our conversation is in heaven.'[461] These armies, that is to say, good and just men, and prelates, follow Jesus, when, for example, they fight the vices in themselves by correction, and in their neighbour by admonition. This is why St James says, 'that he which converteth the sinner

---

[459] Within the Judeo-Christian mysteries the right shoulder is associated with the Logos, the Word, the Transcendent Christ and Wisdom
[460] Revelation 19:14
[461] Philippians 3:20

from the error of his way shall save a soul from death, etc.'[462] These troops mount white horses and are chaste in their bodies.

23. The bodies of the good are called horses, because, just as horses walk according to the will of the rider, so the bodies of the righteous behave according to that of Christ. These horses must be white or covered with white, that is, the bodies of the righteous. And the prelates must be chaste and pure; for if they are not chaste, they cannot follow Christ. Also St Peter said, 'Christ also suffered for us, leaving us an example, that ye should follow his steps, etc.'[463] Clerics of the Holy Roman Church, according to the declaration of the Emperor Constantine mount horses adorned with very bright white covers. In Book Two, in the chapter *The Bishop*, it will be said on which day he is to be consecrated, and why the book of the Gospels is placed on the shoulders of the person to be consecrated. In the seventh place we must speak of the anointing of the altar, of the chalice, and of the other vessels of the church. These are anointed according to custom, when they are dedicated; and this, not only according to the order of the law of God, but also because Moses sprinkled the tabernacle and all the vessels of divine worship with blood. It is also on the example of Blessed Pope Sylvester, who when he consecrated an altar, anointed it with chrism. Now the Lord commanded Moses to make an oil to anoint the tabernacle of the Testimony, the Ark of the Testament, the lampstand, and the vessels, and the other things, as it was said above.[464] These anointings are made on the things that are anointed, that we may have greater respect for them, and that greater grace may be bestowed upon them. These anointings have been spoken of, and will be spoken of in their appropriate places. But the virtue (*sacramentum*) of the anointing produces and represents, of course, another thing, as much in the New as in the Old Testament. That is why the Church does not Judaize when she celebrates the virtue (*sacramentum*) of unction, as some falsely say, some elders who know neither the scriptures nor the power of God. In the chapters devoted to them, we have spoken of the unctions of the church and of the altar.

---

[462] James 5:20
[463] 1 Peter 2:21
[464] See Exodus 30, Exodus 40

CONSECRATIONS AND UNCTIONS

24. Also, the paten is consecrated and anointed, which is used to administer the Body of Christ, who wanted, by the choice that He made, to be sacrificed on the altar of the Cross for the salvation of all. The almighty God ordained that wheat flour should be presented at His altar in patens of gold and silver. The chalice is also consecrated and anointed that the grace of the Holy Spirit may make it a new sepulchre of the Body and Blood of Christ, and that He deigns to sprinkle it with His virtue, He who poured it into the chalice of Melchizedek, His servant.

25. Eighth, we must speak of the extreme unction which, according to the rule instituted by Pope Felix IV and according to the precept of the Apostle St James, those who fight their last struggle are given. Some say, regarding this anointing, that it is not properly a sacrament, which is an anointing made with the chrism on the forehead or elsewhere, because they say, it can be repeated when one prays over a man; which cannot apply to the sacraments. This anointing can be done by one priest, if more cannot be present. By this anointing venial sins are remitted, according to the words of St James, 'Is any sick among you? etc.'[465] as above. Now this anointing is done on the various parts or limbs of the body, and that for the causes that can be gathered from the prayers that are said then. It takes place especially on the members where the five senses of man reside, so that all that the patient has done wrong by them may be erased and destroyed by virtue from this anointing. It is stated by some authors that ordinarily only someone who is at least eighteen should be anointed, and that a patient should be anointed only once in the space of one year, even if there are several phases in the course of his illness, and that no one should be anointed unless, first of all, he has his reason, and has asked for this sacrament either by words or by signs. Again, they should not anoint their shoulders, because they were anointed at baptism, and they are now deprived of their office. One who has been confirmed should not be anointed on the forehead, but on the temples; and the priest's hands should not be anointed on the inside, but on the outside, since they were anointed on the inside during his ordination. Also because he has been anointed once by the bishop, he must not,

---

[465] James 5:14

out of respect for him, be anointed again by a priest. Now if the anointed patient recovers, wash the places of his body where the oil has been shed, and this water should be thrown into the fire. But if he dies, his body will not be washed because of the recent anointing. If the patient is on the verge of death, he will be hastily anointed, in case he dies without having been anointed. There are also certain men who, by a spirit of penance, on the point of dying, put on sackcloth and lie down on the ashes, as will be said in Book Six, when we speak of Ash Wednesday.

26. Ninth, the cemetery, which enjoys the same privileges as the church, is consecrated and blessed, as the Lord blessed, by the hands of his servants Abraham, Isaac and Jacob, the land they had purchased to the sons of Ebron to serve for their burial. Now it is blessed so that henceforth this place may cease to be the habitation of unclean spirits, and that the bodies of the faithful may rest in peace until the Day of Judgment, unless the bodies of the Gentiles are buried therein or the unbelievers, or even excommunicates; and then we bless it only after throwing them out of there.

27. It is also to be noted that the altar linen (*palloe* from which comes 'pall'), the sacerdotal vestments and the ecclesiastical ornaments of all kinds are to be blessed. For we read that Moses, according to the precept of the Lord, consecrated the tabernacle by holy prayers, both the table and the altar, and the vessels and utensils necessary for the fulfilment of the divine worship. If, then, the Jews, who were slaves, did so in 'the law having a shadow of good things to come,'[466] how much more should we, to whom the truth was manifested by Christ, do this and have the vases of divine worship consecrated by the bishop and not by the priests. This is why we read in Exodus, in the penultimate chapter. 'Moses blesses all the vessels necessary for the service of worship.'[467] And, if we add a small piece or fringe to the garment, it is proved by the testimony of the law that we do not need to repeat the blessing. Then, of course, we conclude why these various things are blessed from the form their blessing takes. But we will speak about the sacred garments in the *Preface* to Book

---

[466] Hebrews 10:1
[467] See Exodus 39:43

CONSECRATIONS AND UNCTIONS

Three. Now it should be noted taken that when consecrating the church, and priestly vestments and other ornaments, it is not assumed that they in themselves are capable of receiving grace, since they are inanimate, but because by doing this we know that grace is attached to them. For, like men, so these things, by the blessing and consecration given to both, are made fit for divine worship, and become capable of exercising, and at last inspiring greater veneration. Grace is made more abundant in people, by anointing and blessing. There are some who raise their hands by blessing the ornaments. We will talk about this in the Book Two, in the chapter *The Deacon*. Tenth, this would be the place to speak of the consecration of virgin; but we will deal with this in the *Preface* to Book Two.

9 THE SACRAMENTS OF THE CHURCH

1. With regard to the sacraments of the Church, it should be noted that, according to St Gregory, 'A *sacrament* takes place on some solemn occasion, when an outward act is accomplished in such a way that we receive something of that which it represents, something that we must receive in a holy and dignified way.' The word 'mystery' means that the Holy Spirit operates in a hidden and invisible manner, so that it sanctifies by its operating and blesses by its sanctification.
2. Now, we say 'mystery' when it comes to the sacraments, and 'ministry' when speaking of ornaments. According to St Augustine, the sign of the sacrament is the visible form of the invisible grace. The visible sacrifice is also an invisible sacrament. The sign is also the thing, because of its appearance which it presents to the senses and by means of which it makes known to us the other thing that it contains.
3. The representation of a holy thing (*sacrae rei signum*) or a sacred secret (*sacrum secretum*) is also called sacrament. We shall speak of this in Book Four, in the chapter *The Sixth Part of the Canon*, when considering the words 'Mystery of faith' (*Mysterium fidei*), and in the chapter *The Oblation of the Priest*.
4. Now there are certain sacraments which are only of necessity, others of dignity and necessity at the same time, some of order and necessity, some of dignity and choice, and some of choice only. The sacrament of necessity only is baptism, which, in a supreme need, may be conferred by anyone (though in the form desired by the Church), is helpful for salvation. And it is called of necessity, because without it no one can be saved, if he neglects it out of contempt. We will speak of this sacrament in Book Six,

in the chapter *Holy Saturday*. The sacrament of dignity and necessity is Confirmation. It is of Christian dignity as this sacrament is conferred by the bishop alone. It is at the same time of necessity, because whoever abandons it out of contempt is not saved, as has been said above. We will talk about it on the above-mentioned Saturday. The sacraments of order and necessity are Penance, the Eucharist and Extreme Unction; they are called 'by order,' because they must be given only by those who are, according to the Canons of the Church, raised in dignity, and according to the powers possessed by the Church to open and to close.

5. They must be conferred only in case of necessity; and, in this circumstance, someone may even confess to a layman. They are of necessity, because whoever neglects them with contempt cannot be saved. Concerning Penance, see in Book Six, in the chapter *The Office of the Mass of Holy Thursday*, and what we have said in our *Repertorium*.[468] We will speak of the Eucharist in Book Four and we have spoken of Extreme Unction in the previous chapter.

6. The sacrament of dignity and choice is orders. Of dignity because it is conferred by bishops alone and one must raise and receive there only someone who worthy of it. Of choice, because without it one can be saved. It will be discussed in the *Preface* to Book Two.

7. Marriage is the sacrament of choice alone, and it is called choice, because without it one can be saved, and it is not necessary for the man who wants to come to the kingdom of heaven to marry. Regarding this sacrament, it is to be noted that, according to the Canon, the solemnity of the wedding must not take place from Septuagesima Sunday, which is a time of sorrow, until the Octave of Easter, nor during the three weeks before the feast of St John the Baptist. But, according to the general practice of the Catholic Church,[469] marriage has been publicly contracted

---

[468] *Repertorium iuris canonici* (*Breviarium aureum*), another important work of Durandus. This is a collection of citations from canonists on questions of controversy,

[469] Catholic here can be understood in the sense of universal Church, which today means those denominations which hold that their teachings follow the

in the Church from the day after Low Sunday, that is, from the eighth day of Easter to the first Rogation Day.[470] From the morning on the first day of the Rogations we finish this celebration, and the prohibition lasts until the eighth day after Pentecost inclusively. Here is what Pope Clement says about it in his decretal,[471] 'From the first Sunday of Advent to the Epiphany, we must not celebrate weddings, as he has been said in the aforesaid chapter; and they would not have been allowed until the Octave of the Epiphany, if the Lord had not honoured the wedding[472] with his presence and had not enriched them with a miracle.' That is why at this time we sing, 'Today the Church was united to the Heavenly Spouse.' Some, however, say that it is more correct for this prohibition to extend to the Octave of the same feast, and also that the Office of changing the water into wine should be sung at weddings. Now, in the times enumerated above, one does not contract marriages, because these times are consecrated to prayer.

8. Therefore, a man must separate himself from his wife's bed; as generally the time before the wedding is also a time of abstinence from conjugal embrace, except, perhaps because of the fragility of human nature a man requires a conjugal debt of obligation from his wife or vice versa, which they demand to be paid. For, according to the Apostle, 'The wife hath not power of her own body, but the husband: and likewise also the husband hath not power of his own body, but the wife.'[473] But, although the solemnity of the marriage is forbidden in the aforesaid times, however, the marriage which has been contracted at some other time, by word and in a lawful manner, holds from that moment on. Now, what has been established by the Canon, namely, that the marriage must not be celebrated during the three weeks preceding the feast of Blessed John the Baptist, has been done for

---

line of Apostolic succession. This means that bishops represent a direct, uninterrupted line of continuity from the Apostles of Jesus Christ

[470] The Rogation Days are four days set apart to bless the fields, and ask for God's mercy on all of creation. April 25 (coincidentally the Feast of St Mark) is called the Major Rogation; the three days preceding Ascension Thursday are called the Minor Rogations

[471] A 'decretal' is a papal decree concerning a point of Canon Law

[472] At Cana

[473] 1 Corinthians 7:4

the following reason. It is so that we can go more freely to prayer. For the Church had first instituted two fasting periods, in addition to the main one. One before the birth of the Lord, which is commonly called St Martin[474], and which lasted from his day[475] until Christmas; the other forty days before the feast of blessed John the Baptist, during which time prayer, alms, and fasts were to be performed. However because of the fragility of men, these two seasons were reduced to one. This one was again divided into the three weeks of Advent, and the three before birth of St John the Baptist, during which we must eat and abstain from marriage.

9. According to Blessed Isidore, on the same subject, women are veiled while being married, so that they know that they must always be subject to their husbands. This is why Rebekah, on seeing Isaac, veiled herself. It is for this reason that spouses, after the nuptial blessing, are joined to one another by the bond of a ribbon, so that they do not break the union, that is, the faith of the conjugal union. This strip, is of white and purple cloth, because the whiteness signifies purity of life, and the purple the lawful raising of offspring, so that by this sign, they are reminded at times that they need to practice temporary self-control in order to devote themselves to fasting and prayer.

10. Also the ring which the husband gives to the bride signifies mutual respect, the love of choice; and this is especially done so that by this pledge, that is to say by this sign, their hearts are joined. The ring is placed on the fourth finger, because there is in it a certain vein (as some say) which goes to the heart, the source of blood. Protheus, a certain sage, was the first who established a ring of iron as a token of love; and it is enclosed and as hard as flint, and from there he instituted the pledge of spouses.

11. For just as iron tames everything, so love conquers all things; because there is nothing more vehement than the delirium of love. Also, just as one cannot break a magnet, so one cannot separate two hearts united by love. Because the love of choice is as strong as death.[476] This is why Protheus established the custom of wearing the ring on the ring finger, from which a vein proceeds to the heart. Then the rings of iron were replaced by rings of gold,

---

[474] Martin of Tours
[475] November 11
[476] See Song of Songs 8:6

and, instead of a magnet, they were adorned with precious stones, because, just as the gold prevails over the other metals, so love steps above all good things. Again, as a gem adorns gold, so all virtues enhance marital love. Nuptials, according to St Ambrose, take their name from *nubere* (veiling). Because those who marry (*nubunt*) are accustomed to veiling (*obnubere*) the head out of respect and to remain silent. This is why Rebekah, having seen Isaac, to whom she was to be united, began to veil her head.[477] Modesty must precede the marriage, especially as modesty is a greater guarantee for the marriage itself, and the woman must appear to have more desire for the man than the man for her. According to St Jerome, 'Legitimate marriages are free of sin; however the Holy Spirit is not given at the time of the conjugal act, even if it is a prophet who fulfils the duty of procreation.'[478]

12. It should also be noted that a triple mystery is identified in the carnal consummation of a marriage. The first mystery is the spiritual union of the soul with God by faith, love, and charity, which is the union of the will; which consists of one spirit of love between God and the just soul; which made the Apostle say, 'he that is joined unto the Lord is one spirit.'[479] This mystery is represented by the union of spirits that took place during the first engagement of carnal marriage. The second mystery is the union of human nature with God, which took place in the womb of a Virgin, by the incarnation of the Word of God. Or the conformity of nature, according to the flesh, between Christ and the holy Church; to which this word relates, 'The Word was made flesh, etc.'[480] This mystery is represented by a union of bodies in the carnal consummation of a marriage; it does not mean the union itself, in which the Holy Spirit is not present, but it is to designate, by means of the act itself, what is signified in the consummation. The third mystery is the unity of the Church, composed of the gathering of all nations and subject to one spouse, who is Christ. This mystery has its image in the man who had only one wife, and one virgin woman, and then became a cleric, and was ordained a priest.

---

[477] See Genesis 24:65
[478] The Latin of this quotation is unclear
[479] 1 Corinthians 6:17
[480] John 1:14

13. Therefore, as soon as a man goes to bigamy or a second marriage, he withdraws from that moment of unity, because his flesh is then divided. Thus the representation of this third mystery ceases to exist in him, because he cannot be elevated to the priesthood; for if he were raised there, he could not be the image of that unity of which we have spoken. Moreover, he retires, by a second marriage, from the first union signified by this sacrament. For the Church, as soon as she joined Christ, never withdrew from Him, nor Christ from her. Therefore, he who has had two wives cannot represent such a unity. This is why he cannot rightly be elevated to the rank of husband of the Church, because of the abandonment he has made of this mystery of which we have spoken above.

14. Note also that, according to the rule formulated by the Council of Carthage the bride and bridegroom who are to be blessed must be presented at the church, to the priest , by the parents or bridesmen. After having received the marriage blessing, out of reverence to virginity, they do not consummate the marriage till the next day.

15. Moreover, the wedding must be blessed by the priest with prayers and offerings, according to the rule of Pope Evaristus.[481] But, however, if a man or a woman pass to bigamy by contracting marriage, their union must not be blessed by the priests, because, as they have been blessed once already, one must not repeat this ceremony for them. So, we should only bless the marriage that a virgin woman contracts with a virgin man, and this for the reason stated in the *Preface* of Book Two. Finally, the priest who has celebrated the blessing of a marriage contracted with a second wife will be suspended from office and benefit, and will be handed over to the Apostolic See; which is known to have introduced the encouragement of continence. According to the custom of certain places, when a man contracts a second virgin wife, the nuptial blessing is reiterated, but the Lord Pope must know of this and approve it. Otherwise, the sacrament is invalid. There are some who say that if men, being united with virgins, were not blessed, when remarrying a second time, they may be blessed at this new union; but, if one blesses the husband and

---

[481] In office from c. 99-107

wife, one must not become carnaliter,[482] however, because of this circumstance, if they marry again, their union will not be blessed. We will speak of the blessing of the virgins in the Preface to Book Two.

16. It is to be remarked that a sacrament is more worthy than another in four ways, namely, because of its efficacy, like baptism; because of its holiness, like the Eucharist; because of its meaning, like marriage, (however some do not approve of this view), and because of the one who confers it, such as Confirmation and Holy Orders.

17. But we ask why the sacraments were instituted, since without them God could have given mankind eternal life and grace? I answer that it is for three reasons. First, for the humiliation of man, so that while the creature submits himself with respect, according to the precept of God, to insensitive and inferior things, he deserves more, by this obedience, before God. Secondly, for his instruction, so that his soul may be instructed by what it sees outside, clothed with a visible appearance of the invisible virtue whose existence she must recognize within herself. Thirdly, to serve him as an exercise, because, as man must not be idle, a useful and salutary exercise is opened to him and proposed in the sacraments, an exercise by the practice of which he will abandon all vain and harmful occupation, according to this word, 'Make always some good work, that the devil may find you busy.' So, we must not omit them, as we said in the previous chapter.

---

[482] A worldly minded man. One addicted to fleshly practices

SCRIPTURE INDEX

Genesis
1:2	103
8:20	33, 101
12:8	33, 101
18:12	54
18:27	90, 103
23:9	76
24:65	136
26:25	33
27:27	114
28:12	40
28:14	105
28:18	91, 112
33:20	33
48:13	89

Exodus
3:5	31
16:33	53
16:33-34	40
20:4	42, 43
20:7-17	4
20:23	43
20:24	34, 36
20:25	34
20:26	34, 40
22:28	3
23:16	19
24:9-10	46
25:5	19
25:6-8	19
25:11	33
25:12	55, 109
25:30-33	63
25:31	35
26:3	124
26:32, 37	24
26:33	16
27:1	111
27:6	33
27:17-19	63
27:20	28
28:4	8
28:22	50
28:30	8
28:33-35	67
29:12	108
30	128
30:3	33
30:18-19	27
30:22-37	117
30:23-25	80
34:33	57
34:33, 35	vii

36	5	**1 Kings**	
39:43	130	2:28	32
40	128	4:20	59
40:20	35, 39	6	80
40:23	40	6:20	33
		6:22	111
Leviticus		8:2-68, 15	109
6:13	38	8:4-5	16
14	97	8:9	35
14:4-7	98	8:30	83
15	97	19:15-16	126
15:31	95	6:22	34
16	116		
21:10	123	**2 Kings**	
26:1	43	18:4	44
26:10	55		
		2 Chronicles	
Numbers		6:13	26
1:47	29		
6:5	48	**Nehemiah**	
24:17	55	4:7	18
		8:4	26
Deuteronomy		**Tobit**	
4:16	43	13:22	102
4:19	44	14:12	79
5:4	2		
5:27	35, 40	**Job**	
22:11	4	19:21	113
32:13	1	31:37	40
		38:33	1
Joshua		39:13	61
5:15	31		
		Psalms	
1 Samuel		2:12	38
9:22-24	126	5:12	51
17:48-50	6	8:5	51

SCRIPTURE INDEX

9:14	87	97:7	43
11:4	16	102:9	103
16:6	61	103:5	48
19:4	21	104:10	1
22:22	107	111:10	106
23:5	37	112:5	114
24:7	87	115:4	43
24:7-8	84	115:8	43
26:8	61	118:19-20	87
27:13	20	118:22	111
30:5	47	118:27	34
34:7	86	119:25	20
34:8	37	119:37	58
45:13	124	119:164	26
45:7	111, 112	120-134	35
45:16	15	122:3	17
50:16	68	127:1	82
51	107	132:8	53
51:17	106, 116	133:2	125
51:19	34	145:9	112
51:7	95		
68	91	**Proverbs**	
68:5	91	9:1	24
68:6	13	25:21	6
69:23	2	31:18	38
75:8	62	31:20	125
79:1	95		
80:1	46	**Ecclesiastes**	
84:1	39	2:14	120
84:3	34	9:8	6
84:7	40		
87:1	17	**Song of Songs**	
91	91	1:5	61
92:2	66	1:17	25
92:12	49	2:4	1
95:10-11	3	3:9	25

3:10	24, 25, 28	55:1	106
		60:1	54
3:11	50	61:1	28
4:4	22		
5:5	124	**Jeremiah**	
5:7	105	8:6	113
8:6	92, 135	9:24	110
8:7	38	31:15	15
		51:7	62
Wisdom			
10:21	2	**Lamentations**	
14:11	44	4:4	37
15:3	110		
		Ezekiel	
Ecclesiasticus		1:10	47
3:20	25	1:16	89
18:12	113	3:8	67
24:21	125	3:26	72
30:24	113	4:1	44
33:29	38	8:9	44
35:6	38		
47:10-11	101	**Daniel**	
		2:34	111
		3:2	81
Isaiah		5	64
2:3	112		
6:1	46	**Jonah**	
6:2	46	3:6	103
6:5	113		
9:6	126	**Habakkuk**	
10:27	112	2:20	16
11:1	5		
11:2	28	**Malachi**	
11:4	87	2:2	100
12:3	1		
24:2	2	**Matthew**	
53:3-5	63	5:3	25

5:7-8	vii	8:1	2
5:8	6	10:1	23
5:13	85	10:5	88
5:14	28	10:34	123
5:16	28, 114	11:9-10,	ii
5:44	111	11:33	37, 55
6:17	112, 124	11:34	37
7:24	16	12:42	vi
8:17	63	16:29	45
13:11	57	17:10	113
15:14	2	19:14	111
15:32	38	21:27	46
16:18	110	22:17	62
16:24	21	22:19	101
19:17	20	22:61	61
20:22	62		
21:13	91, 107	**John**	
22:40	39	1:1	47
23:4	121	1:9	27
23:5	54	1:14	136
25:1	50	1:17	81
25:20	114	1:29	45
25:31, 33	48	3:5	85, 103
25:34	115	3:29	15
26:9	63	4:11	1
28:18	46	7:38	103
		8:12	27, 49
Mark		8:59	56
1:4	104	10:9	24
9:50	85	14:2	29
16:18	118	14:6	7, 49
28:19	90	14:23	21
		15:5	81, 102
Luke		17:17	88
2:10-11	54	19:30	89
4:18	125		

Acts
4:27 126
8:36-38 104

Romans
1:17 110, 119
2:13 109
5:5 110
5:20 v
8:35 115
10:10 119

1 Corinthians
2:2 92
3:1-2 vi
3:17 106
6:17 136
7:4 134
8:4 44
9:27 22, 68
10:4 107
10:13 30
11:1 109
11:5 31
12:8 112
12:8-10 52
12:11 2
13:1 67
13:2-8 39
13:13 56
15:28 29

2 Corinthians
1:12 114, 123
2:14 115
2:15 124, 126
2:16 124
3:15 57
11:2 15

Galatians
2:2 69
2:9 24
5:6 119
6:10 125
6:14 68

Ephesians
2:14 55
2:20 17, 110
4:11 49
5:8 54
5:14 22, 70
5:19 31
5:23 31, 126
6:14, 16, 17 19

Philippians
2:7 60
2:9 111
2:10 66
3:20 127

Colossians
2:3 63
4:6 85

1 Timothy
3:7 124

Hebrews
1:9 114, 126
7:12 4
9:4 35

10:1	130	**1 John**	
11:6	110	2:17	16
13:10	106	2:27	118
13:14	16	3:18	6

James		**Revelation**	
1:5	1	3:5	49
2:13	113	3:7	1
2:26	119	4:4	47
5:14	129	5:4-5	49
5:14-15	118	7:14	6
5:20	128	10:1-2	31
		12:7	46
1 Peter		14:13	75
2:9	119	19:14	127
2:21	128	21:16	20
3:15	120	22:14	6
4:8	20, 110	22:17	124
4:11	23		

2 Peter

2:19	v

SUBJECT INDEX

A

abbot   49, 77
ablution   90
abstinence   134
adultery   78, 97
allegorical   4, 5, 7, 9, 68
alphabet   84, 88, 89, 90
ambo   26
Ambrose   136
anagogical   4, 5, 6, 7, 9
angel   6, 21, 31, 34, 43, 46, 48, 49, 54, 86, 102, 116, 126
    angelic   6
    archangel   46
Apostolic   7, 137
apse   22
arches   25
Arians   82
Arnaud   122
aspersion   96, 104, 116
    aspersory   101, 107
Augustine   3, 7, 8, 77, 119, 120, 132

B

baluster   26, 29
banner   53, 56, 91
baptistery   65
basilica   14, 36
beam   25, 97
Bede   30
bell   66
Boethius   4
bow   42, 66, 105
breastplate   8, 19, 50
bride   15, 22, 25, 135, 137
bridegroom   15, 22, 59, 137
Burchard   59, 81

C

candle   37, 38, 83, 116
candlestick   35, 36, 37, 38, 53, 54, 55, 63, 64
Canonical Hours   26
catechumens   88, 116, 118
chain   68, 75, 99
chancel   19, 20
chapel   14, 77
cherubim   46, 109
Chrysostom   31
Church Militant   14, 16, 23, 34, 71
Church Triumphant   7, 14, 29, 34
circumcision   4, 106, 119
clock   26, 70
cloister   28, 29, 70, 73
cock   22, 23, 45
column   23, 24, 29
communion of saints   15
confessor   30, 49, 53, 108, 114
Confirmation   115, 120, 122, 133, 138
Constantine   36, 128
convent   14
Council
    Agathensian   45
    Carthage   82, 137

Lerida	64
Lyon	41
Mainz	29
Mayence	79
Orleans	64
Reims	61
Toledo	40
crosier	55, 87
crown	21, 47, 50, 51, 69, 106, 121
corona	21
crypt	22
cushion	53
cymbal	67, 70

D

Dead, Office for	9, 78, 79
door	1, 20, 24, 45, 58, 64, 83, 84, 87, 88, 98
dragon	46

E

eagle	45, 47, 48
east	17, 55, 89, 90, 105
eternal life	5, 17, 25, 124, 138
exedra	22
exorcise	86, 93, 95, 96, 98, 102

F

fast	38, 58, 59, 60, 135
Faustinus	76
firstfruits	19
five senses	23, 114, 115, 129
Flavianus	21
font	116

G

garden	30, 106
gate	6, 22, 57, 83, 87, 88
Gentiles	17, 42, 44, 54, 70, 74, 89, 90, 130
Gilbert	105

H

historical	4
host	34, 39, 44, 53, 123, 125
husband	15, 31, 134, 135, 137, 138
hyssop	83, 85, 86, 95, 101, 107

I

Ignatius	21
incense	19, 27, 33, 44, 102, 109, 114, 115
Isidore	135

J

Jerome	4, 76, 136

L

lamp	27, 28, 36, 37, 40, 47, 50, 55, 92, 116
lattice	23
litanies	84, 88
literal	23

M

marriage	84, 133, 134, 135, 136, 137, 138, *See* nuptual
Martin, of Tours	135
martyr	14, 30, 49, 53, 77, 108, 114
martyrium	14
Matins	70, 71
Michael	46
misericord	25
moral sense	29
mortification	34, 37, 39, 59, 105
mystical	4, 5, 6, 8, 19, 23, 115, 116
mystically	25

N

nave	20, 52
Night Office	70, 71
Nimshi	126
None	70
nuptial	64, 135, 136, *See* marriage

SUBJECT INDEX

O

oratory	15, 30, 96

P

pall	64, 130
pallium	52
pavement	20, 24, 25, 53, 65, 78, 84, 88, 89, 90
penance	27, 103, 104, 130, 133
Pope	61
Adrian	45
Alexander	110
Boniface	99
Clement	64, 134
Evaristus	137
Felix	81, 129
Gelasius	116
Gregory	38, 42, 44, 50, 51, 67, 69, 76, 82, 83, 95, 96, 124
Martin	59
Nicholas	92
Pelagius	92
Sabinian	69
Stephen	64
Sylvester	36, 121, 128
Urban	61
porch	22, 73
Prime	29, 69, 70
procession	71, 109
pulpit	26, 82

Q

Quadragesima	70

R

Rabanus	120, 122
relics	35, 54, 82, 93, 101, 108, 109, 110
Richard of St Victor	19
rood	42
roof	14, 20, 26, 72, 83, 92, 97, 98

S

sacristy	27, 64
salt	83, 84, 85, 96, 102, 103, 104
sanctuary	14, 16, 19, 20, 25, 26, 56, 57, 58, 116
Sebastian	82
Septuagesima	133
seraphim	46
serpent	44
Sext	70
shield	19, 51
Sicard	28, 121
spouse	86, 134, 135, 136
staff	83, 87, 88, 90, 127
stall	25, 26
Stephen	49

T

tapestries	15
Terce	69, 70
Testament	35, 36, 39, 40, 80, 109, 117, 128
New	67, 119
Old	19, 27, 56, 57, 92, 97, 108, 123, 126
Testaments	
Old and New	47, 52, 55, 62, 67, 89, 108, 128
Theodorus	21
tiles	26
Titus	36
tomb	74, 75, 76, 79, 93, 102
tongs	55
tower	22, 68, 70
tropological	4, 7, 9
tropology	6

V

vault	22, 52, 74, 76, 77
Vespers	58, 70, 71
vessel	62, 64, 95, 128, 130
Vigilantius	54
virgin	15, 20, 27, 30, 50, 53, 86, 111, 114, 117, 131, 136, 137, 138
virginity	137

BOOK ONE

W

wheel	89	wife	31
widow	15, 18	window	21, 23, 45, 58
		womb	18, 45, 105, 136

This translation of the
RATIONALE DIVINORUOM OFFICIORUM
Consists of the following volumes:

Volume 1
Author's Preface
Book 1 - The Church and its Parts

Volume 2
Book 2 - Ministers, Ecclesiastical Dignities and their Duties
Book 3 - The Sacred Vestments

Volume 3
Book 4 - The Mass and its Mysteries

Volume 4
Book 5 -The Divine Offices

Volume 5
Book 6 - The Liturgical Year

Volume 6
Book 7 - The Festivals of Saints
Book 8 - Computation and the Calendar

Volume 7 – The Indices

IN HIS PREFACE TO BOOK TWO DURANDUS WRITES:

1. In this second book we intend to treat of the ministers and dignities of the Church, and of their duties. In principle, we shall lay down that there are three principle sects,[483] namely, the Gentiles, the Hebrews, and the Christians. The first is a sect of error; the second, of truth; the third, of truth and salvation. In the first we are shipwrecked; in the second, we are torn from the peril; in the third, we are saved. The first sect (*secta*) derives its name from *sectare* (cut off), because it subtracts us, that is, separates us from God; the second and third sects, in a similar way, are called *secta*, from *sectare* (seek and possess), because they enlighten, save and deliver. Both the secular and the ecclesiastical among the Christians are taken from the two other sects, which are Hebrew and pagan. Now, just as there are two kinds of people among us, namely, the laity and the ecclesiastics, so it was with the Gentiles and the Hebrews.

2. Among the Gentiles, the secular people were the monarch or the Roman emperor; the patricians, who were also called senators, according to which everything was ordered; kings, dukes, counts, governors, prefects, suffrages, tribunes of soldiers, tribunes of the people, praetors, centurions, decurions, quarteniers, decemvirs, quaestors, aediles and ushers of the palace. Among the literary inventers were advocates, epic poets, historiographers in verse, comedians, tragedians and historiographers in prose.[484]

3. The word *vates*, which comes from *vi mentis* (the transport of the soul), sometimes means the priest, sometimes the prophet, sometimes the poet. According to St Isidore,[485] the Gentiles, in

---

[483] *Secta*, Durandus says; is to conform to the strict word for word that we translate *secta* by *sect*. Here, this word has the meaning of *part, portion*, and not of *sect* in the mystical sense of the branches separated from the nutrient trunk of the tree of life

[484] Praetors (moneylenders), centurions, decurions, and quarteniers, (army officers) decemvirs (law makers), quaestors (public investigators), aediles (responsible for public order and maintenance of public buildings).

[485] Saint Isidore of Seville, (c. 560–636), a scholar and, for over three decades, Archbishop of Seville, is widely regarded as the last of the Fathers of the Church

the order of the ceremonies of the temple, counted the archiflamines,[486] the protoflamines, the flamines, and the priests, as will soon be said. There were also religious convent communities of men and women.

4. Among the Hebrews there also existed the same diversity of people; for some were secular, and others consecrated to divine worship in the temple. In the temple there was the high priest, like Melchizedek; the priests of an inferior Orders, the Levites; the Nethinim,[487] those who extinguished the lights; the exorcists, the doorkeepers and the elect or cantors.

---

[486] In ancient Roman religion a *flamine* was a priest assigned to one of fifteen deities

[487] Mentioned in the books of Ezra, Nehemiah and Chronicles the Nethinim were the servants or slaves entrusted by the priests with subordinate labours in the Temple of Jerusalem

IN HIS PREFACE TO BOOK THREE DURANDUS WRITES:

1. We must not use sacred vestments as usual garments, because, as we change our clothes according to the letter, so we must act according to the spirit. Therefore, we will not enter the Holy of Holies with the dirty clothes of the common life; but we must touch the sacraments of God with a pure conscience and chaste and consecrated clothing. Regarding this Pope Stephen decided that sacred clothing should be used only in ecclesiastical ceremonies and at the Offices celebrated in honour of God. Also Ezekiel said that they should not bless the people by wearing their vestments outside of the temple.[488] There is therefore one set of clothes for divine religion, for the Offices of the Church, and another for the ordinary use of life. The purpose of this is to show to all Christian people the example of a good life, and how, after having first washed away their defilements, they become new men in the eyes of Christ. Indeed, the priest strips off the old man by his deeds, and then puts on the new one, which was created according to God.[489] By the clothes also, which we use only to celebrate the holy mysteries, we mean that we must not reveal them all to the people.[490] It should be observed that in the time of Louis, Emperor, son of Charles the Great,[491] the bishops and clerics laid down their belts of gold, their exquisite, and the other ornaments of the age.

2. The sacred clothes seem to have been taken from the old law; for the Lord commanded Moses to make holy garments for

---

[488] See Ezekiel 44:19
[489] See Colossians 3:9-10
[490] There have always been many mysteries in the Christianity that have only been revealed to those who are spiritually prepared and ready to receive them. The *Divine Rationale* opens the door to some of these and, as found in the writings of the Fathers, points to others for those who have eyes to see. Jesus Himself (Matt 13:11, Luke 8:10) indicated that this was ever the case. There is a teaching which says that all is open and revealed within Christianity but this is true only in the sense that all teachings are *available* to anyone. There are many things which are not properly understood but this does not mean that a sound understanding of them does not exist
[491] Louis the Pious, 778–840

Aaron the priest and for his sons, to glorify Him and to honour Him,[492] so that after washing and putting on their vestments they should perform their work in the ceremonies.[493] The Lord also instructed Moses, for forty days, to make the pontifical and sacerdotal vestments for his priests and Levites, and also adornments for the linen clothes. Miriam wove and did what was to be used for ministry in the tabernacle of the Covenant; and Ecclesiasticus says, 'to the festivals he added beauty, etc.'[494] There are, however, vestments borrowed from the Apostles but these are those which mark the virtues of the virtues of the mystery of the Incarnation.

---

[492] See Exodus 28:2
[493] See Exodus 40:12-13
[494] Ecclesiasticus 47:12

IN HIS PREFACE TO BOOK FOUR DURANDUS WRITES:

1. Of all the mysteries (*sacramenta*) of the Church, it is agreed that the one which is of the greatest importance is the Office of the Mass which is celebrated on the most holy altar. This mystery is the feast of the Church in which the father kills the fatted calf to celebrate the return of His Son,[495] and where He offers the bread of life and wine mixed with wisdom.[496]

2. However, it is Christ himself who instituted the Office, when He concluded the New Testament,[497] by sharing His kingdom with His heirs, as His father had arranged with Him, so they eat and drink on His table in His kingdom.[498] It is for this that the Church has been consecrated. For, as they ate supper, Jesus took bread and giving thanks, blessed and broke it, and gave it to His disciples, saying, 'This is my body which is given for you: this do in remembrance of me.'[499] So the Apostles, formed by this teaching, began to frequently offer the most holy mystery for the reasons that Christ had expressly indicated. They keep the same form in the words and the same material in species[500] and as the Apostle says to the Corinthians, 'For I have received of the Lord that which also I delivered unto you, That the Lord Jesus the same night in which he was betrayed took bread: And when he had given thanks, he brake it, and said, Take, eat: this is my body, etc.'[501] Therefore, the Office of the Mass is more dignified and solemn than the rest of the Divine Offices. That is why we must speak of it in this Fourth Book before the other Offices. We will

---

[495] See Luke 15:23
[496] See Proverbs 9:1-2
[497] The New Testament is normally considered to end with the book of Revelation. However the *new testimony* or *new testament* which Jesus presented ended at the Last Supper.
[498] See Luke 22:29-30
[499] Luke 22:19
[500] Or in kind.
[501] 1 Corinthians 11:23-25

also consult the *Speculum* of Pope Innocent III,[502] with regards to some mysteries and some points which have been attacked by heretics.

---

[502] In office from 1198-1216

IN HIS PREFACE TO BOOK FIVE DURANDUS WRITES:

1. It is written in Exodus that the Lord said to Moses, 'And look that thou make them after their pattern, which was shewed thee in the mount.'[503] That is why we must conform ourselves to that heavenly Jerusalem which was commanded to praise the Lord, and which, as the Apostle says to the Galatians, 'But Jerusalem which is above…is the mother of us all,'[504] but above all, at all times, in praising God, according to these words, 'I have set watchmen upon thy walls, O Jerusalem, which shall never hold their peace day nor night.'[505] And in the Apocalypse it is said that the animals, 'rest not day and night, saying, Holy, holy, holy, etc.'[506] However, the Church Militant cannot completely imitate the Church Triumphant; for as it is read in the book of Wisdom, 'For the corruptible body is a load upon the soul.'[507] Therefore precluded in advance by our infirmity, we cannot, at every hour of the day, continually celebrate the divine praises, because it is necessary for man, from time to time, to supply the needs of the body, according to these words of Genesis, 'In the sweat of thy face shalt thou eat bread.'[508] That is why we do what we can, by praising God at certain hours of the natural day.

2. Therefore on returning from the captivity of Babylon the prophet Ezra taught the people of Israel to praise God four times during the night and four times during the day, so that man offered himself and his work to the Creator for a number of hours equal to the number of the four elements that make up his body. In this way he could fittingly offer his allegiance to God at the appropriate hours, that is to say during the night at Vespers,

---

[503] Exodus 25:40
[504] Galatians 4:26
[505] Isaiah 62:6
[506] Revelation 4:8
[507] Wisdom 9:15
[508] Genesis 3:19

Compline, and the Night Office,[509] then at daybreak following with Lauds and Matins, and then during the day, the hours of Prime, Terce, Sext, and None. Now, it is proved that Vespers, which is the start of all the Offices, and which, according to St Isidore, gets its name from, *vespera stella*, or the, 'evening star,' which appears at the approach of night, belongs to the night. But David said, 'Seven times a day do I praise thee,'[510] and then, 'At midnight I will rise to give thanks unto thee, etc.'[511] This order was approved by the Council of Agde,[512] and is preserved by the Holy Church, since the Night Office is sung in the middle of the night. The other seven Canonical Hours are said to be of the day, namely, Lauds and Matins, which are linked and said at dawn, then, Prime, Terce, Sext, None,[513] Vespers, and Compline. These seven hours are called 'Canonical,' as if they are said to be, 'regular,' because the holy Fathers regularly observed them

---

[509] For clarity, 'Night Office,' will indicate the Office held in the middle of the night and, 'night Offices,' will be used to refer to Vespers, Compline, the Night office, Lauds and Matins
[510] Psalm 110:164
[511] Psalm 119:62
[512] A.D. 506
[513] Prime, Terce, Sext, None, are Latin words which, respectively, mean First, Third, Sixth and Ninth

IN HIS PREFACE TO BOOK SIX DURANDUS WRITES:

1. In the preceding part of this work, which we now leave, we have treated of the Divine Offices in general; now we will take them in particular and show them in their diversity throughout the course of the year. Thus, we will review the Sunday services, a few week days, the solemnities of the Lord, and the fasts of the ember days;[514] we will see the agreement of the same Offices,[515] both those of the night and those of the Mass. We will not speak only of those of one church but will endeavour to treat the Offices of various churches. For the better understanding of this work, we will begin by considering the distinctions of time. The solar year includes the succession of the four seasons, that is to say, the winter season when the fields are sown, then spring when the seeds grow and elongate into spikes. Next comes the summer when the crops bleach and fall under the edge of the scythe and finally autumn, when the grain, separated from its envelope by the winnower, is put in reserve in the attics. Now the great year of the present life, which extends from the beginning of the centuries to the end of the world, is also measured by four different ages.

2. The first is an age of degeneration in the human race. It extends from Adam to Moses. At that time men gave up the worship of God, who is the true light, and they became idolaters, no longer preserving the shadow of the light of true doctrine. Of that time we read that, 'They are corrupt, they have done abominable works, there is none that doeth good.'[516] Then man abandons his Creator, and, addressing a rough stone, he says to it, 'You are my god.' This time of ignorance and blindness goes well with winter, where darkness reigns.

3. The second age is that of recall or renovation. It extends from Moses to the Nativity of Christ. At that time men are instructed,

---

[514] Four separate sets of three days within the same week, (more precisely, the Wednesday, Friday, and Saturday) roughly equidistant in the circuit of the year, that are set aside for fasting and prayer
[515] Services
[516] Psalm 14:1

by the law and the prophets, of the coming of Christ, the forgiveness of sins, and the love of one God. Then the Lord said to Israel, 'Hear, O Israel: The Lord our God is one Lord: And thou shalt love the Lord thy God with all thine heart, and with all thy soul, and with all thy might.'[517] So man then knew his duties to himself, to God, and to his neighbour. God, afterwards and for the same reason, raised up the prophets, so that their preaching might bring man back increasingly from his errors. This time coincides with spring, which possesses some light mingled with much darkness.

---

[517] Deuteronomy 6:4-5

IN HIS PREFACE TO BOOK SEVEN DURANDUS WRITES:

1. Having first spoken of the Divine Offices in general, the Sunday services and the Lord's festivities in particular, it is useful for us to add something about the Offices of the saints' festivities in this seventh book. Certainly, the Church celebrates the feasts of the saints for many reasons. First, so that we may reciprocate; for they themselves celebrate feasts concerning us, since the angels of God and the souls of the saints experience great joy in heaven, 'over one sinner that repenteth.'[518] Secondly, because by honouring them we do our own proper actions, for their feast is ours too, hence the Apostle says, 'all are yours; And ye are Christ's.'[519] Thirdly, that they may intercede in our favour, which comes from reading in the third book of Kings[520] that Beersheba, which by interpretation means, 'the well of satiety,' that is to say, the Church Triumphant, obtained the kingdom for her son. Fourth, so that we may imitate them, for their examples excite us to imitate them. Fifth, to increase our security and raise our hope. For if men, mortals like us, could have been brought up so high by their merits, we could rise in the same way; because, 'the Lord's hand is not shortened.'[521] Sixthly, to honour the divine majesty whom we honour in the saints, when we honour them, and when we proclaim admirable the One who sanctified them. Seventhly, so that at the sight of their beauty and purity man remains confounded, looking back at his own sins, and disdains the goods of the earth, as they did themselves.

2. The eighth and principal reason is that we recall the memory of the saints on the anniversary of their honour, for our own benefit, because in them we honour God. For, as they are perfectly happy, they do not need our prayers, since they have every wish; moreover, it is an insult to a martyr when one prays for him.

---

[518] Luke 15:7
[519] 1 Corinthians 3:22-23
[520] 1 Kings 1 First and Second Samuel are also called first and second books of Kings, First and second Kings then become third and fourth
[521] Isaiah 59:1

3. St John Damascene[522] provides other reasons why we must honour the saints, and also their bodies or relics. Among the reasons he gives, some relate to the dignity of these saints, others relate to the inestimable price of their bodies themselves. They are worthy of our veneration for four reasons; for they are the friends of God and the children of God, the heirs of God and guides to us. Regarding the first reason St John says, 'I call you not servants, etc.'[523] Regarding the second the same saint says, 'to them gave he power to become the sons of God.'[524] Regarding the third, the Apostle says, 'we are the children of God: And if children, then heirs; etc.'[525] Regarding the fourth, it is said, 'If anyone goes out of his way to find a guide who leads him to some mortal king and pleads his cause before this king, how much more must we not honour the guides of the human race, who intercede for us with God, erecting temples and venerating their memory?'

---

[522] St John of Damascus (Book 4, chap. 7)
[523] John 15:15
[524] John 1:12
[525] Romans 8:16-17

IN HIS PREFACE TO BOOK EIGHT DURANDUS WRITES:

1. Priests, as the Blessed Augustine says, are obliged to know the compute, otherwise they would hardly deserve the name of priests. Under this word 'compute' we understand the knowledge of the course of time, the moon and the calendar.

2. Now the compute is a science whose object is to make time known according to the course and the march of the sun and the moon. That is why, in this eighth and last book we shall say, in a clear and concise abstract, a few words of the compute, as we know it is in use in the Church, for the instruction of those priests who are ignorant.

3. The word, 'compute,' comes from 'computations', 'calculating', 'counting', not that in the compute we learn the art of calculating and counting, but because in the compute we proceed by calculating, by the knowledge of arithmetic, which is then both useful and necessary. There are two kinds of computes, namely, the astronomical or philosophical compute, and the vulgar or ecclesiastical compute, but nothing is said now of the astronomical compute. The vulgar compute is the knowledge whose object is to distinguish, or to divide time in a fixed or certain way, or the knowledge which divides time according to the use of the Church.

4. Time here is taken, according to Cicero, for a certain portion or quantity of the year, the month, the day, or some other period. Or again, it is the time or interval that variable things take to execute their movement and to provide their course.

www.ingramcontent.com/pod-product-compliance
Lightning Source LLC
Chambersburg PA
CBHW051646230426
43669CB00013B/2459